ANNABEL GRIFFITHS (bottom) got publicly dumped in a restaurant and promptly became a bittergirl. MARY FRANCIS MOORE (top) is a bittergirl because chocolate is fattening, because she's never had a tan, because he dumped her before she dumped him. ALISON LAWRENCE (middle) was a poor, broken-down single mom until she found salvation in a pair of strappy sandals and a classy evening gown, and wrote *bittergirl* with Annabel and Mary Francis. Collectively, the bittergirls have been dumped fifty-seven times.

In 1999 three women, all writers and actors—one divorced, one just dumped by her longtime live-in, and one facing yet another failed short-term romance—met in Toronto. They decided to start holding weekly writing meetings for inspiration and motivation. Over endless cups of coffee, the talk at the meetings inevitably turned to relationships and bad breakup stories. So the girls took their outrageous, sometimes unbelievable, experiences of getting dumped and, a few meetings and some pretty funny writing later, they realized they had the makings of a play. Quicker than you can say "It's not you, it's me," the smash-hit play *bittergirl* was conceived and the bittergirls were born.

Dressed in snappy black cocktail gowns with martinis in hand (if they were going to write a show sprung from misery, they were going to look good performing it), the bittergirls have toured to London, England, and New York City for showcase performances and have had three successful sold-out runs in Toronto. They've gone from being nodding acquaintances to finishing each other's sentences.

The bittergirls have had drinks named after them and audiences arrive at the show dressed like them, and their exes have lined up to claim the most outrageous dumpings in the show as their own. The bittergirls have been covered extensively in the media, appearing in numerous publications and television shows—everything from *The Toronto Star* to *CBC Newsworld*. They have offered advice on television and radio, in line at the grocery store, and in the waiting room of their OB/GYN. Everywhere they go they hear the same words: "Are you the bittergirls? Well, let me tell you *my* story ..." So it only made sense that the girls sat down with a bottle of wine and decided to share those stories with an even wider audience—they had to write a book and spread the bittergirl gospel.

See what happens when you embrace the bitterness? Empowerment from misery—and a heck of a lot of fun along the way.

BITTERGIRL
GETTING OVER GETTING DUMPED

ANNABEL GRIFFITHS
ALISON LAWRENCE
MARY FRANCIS MOORE

A PLUME BOOK

PLUME
Published by Penguin Group
Penguin Group (USA) Inc., 375 Hudson Street, New York, New York 10014, USA
Penguin Group (Canada), 10 Alcorn Avenue, Toronto,
Ontario M4V 3B2, Canada (a division of Pearson Penguin Canada Inc.)
Penguin Books Ltd., 80 Strand, London WC2R 0RL, England
Penguin Ireland, 25 St. Stephen's Green, Dublin 2, Ireland (a division of Penguin Books Ltd.)
Penguin Group (Australia), 250 Camberwell Road, Camberwell, Victoria 3124,
Australia (a division of Pearson Australia Group Pty. Ltd.)
Penguin Books India Pvt. Ltd., 11 Community Centre, Panchsheel Park,
New Delhi – 110 017, India
Penguin Group (NZ), cnr Airborne and Rosedale Roads, Albany,
Auckland 1310, New Zealand (a division of Pearson New Zealand Ltd.)
Penguin Books (South Africa) (Pty.) Ltd., 24 Sturdee Avenue,
Rosebank, Johannesburg 2196, South Africa

Penguin Books Ltd., Registered Offices: 80 Strand, London WC2R 0RL, England

Published by Plume, a member of Penguin Group (USA) Inc. Previously published in
Canada by Penguin Canada.

First American Printing, September 2005
10 9 8 7 6 5 4 3 2 1

Ⓟ REGISTERED TRADEMARK—MARCA REGISTRADA

LIBRARY OF CONGRESS CATALOGING-IN PUBLICATION DATA

Griffiths, Annabel.
    Bittergirl : getting over getting dumped / Annabel Griffiths, Alison Lawrence,
Mary Francis Moore.
      p. cm.
    ISBN 0-452-28671-9
    1. Man-woman relationships.   2. Separation (Psychology)   3. Single women—
Psychology.   I. Title: Bitter girl. II. Lawrence, Alison, 1959–   III. Moore, Mary
Francis.   IV. Title.
HQ801.G75 2005
306.81'53—dc22   2005042179

Printed in the United States of America

To The Mountie, The Magic Man, and The Coward.
Here's to Happily Ever After . . . without you.

contents

Acknowledgments

Thanks to the fabulous Jackie Joiner and everyone at The Bukowski Agency; to the sassy Julie Saltman and everyone at Plume; to Nicole de Montbrun; to Andrea Crozier and all at Penguin Group (Canada); to Karen Alliston; to Sarah Cooper at The Saint Agency; and to Rick Gerrits and The Core Group.

Thank you to Emma Healey, Brendan Wall, Timothy Fitzsimmons, and Brian Young; and the Moores, the Griffiths, and the Lawrences, for all their love and support.

Thank you to our bitterboys, who were with us through five years of development and performance of *bittergirl,* the play: Michael Waller, John Patrick Robichaud, Stephen Reich, and David Macniven. And to Shauna Japp and Melinda Little, our standby bittergirls.

Thank you to everybody who helped us with the production of *bittergirl,* the play. Without you there would have been no play, and without the play there would have been no book. We've thanked you before, but we can't thank you enough.

And, finally, thank you to all the bittergirls out there who shared their stories with us. You're living, laughing proof that bittergirls are bettergirls.

THE BITTERGIRL MANIFESTO

Everyone has their story.

Some have many stories.

But there's always one:

The one we coin the breakup of all breakups.

And everyone thinks theirs is the most painful.

"Nobody hurt like I did," we say.

We thrive on it, we bond through it.

*And if someone steals our glory, if someone's story surpasses
    the pain and hurt of our tale, we dismiss it.*

Don't dismiss it.

We've all earned our scars.

*Remember, when all hope is lost, when you feel there's no
    tomorrow,*

You're walking in darkness and drowning in sorrow,

Remember,

Yesterday's heartache is tomorrow's one-liner.

We laugh and move on.

It's what we do. It's how we get through.

We've got our stories. What's yours?

one

welcome to the club

HONEY, YOU'VE BEEN DUMPED. It took an hour to get a cab and now you're standing alone in the hallway of your apartment building. You got yourself all dressed up for a big night out at that fancy restaurant the two of you had been dying to try, and here you are with mascara running down your face and a huge run in your stockings. That's the last time you pay fifteen bucks for a pair of fishnets. You can't find your keys. Oh my God, did you really take the tablecloth and all its contents with you as you fled to the bathroom? How are you going to get that Shiraz stain out of your cashmere twin set? Where *are* those damn keys? Can your neighbors hear your sobs? Did they know He was leaving? How are you going to go in to work tomorrow? Why is there a pepper shaker in your purse? Are you a kleptomaniac? Great, now you're single and a fugitive from the law. How are you going to get through the rest of your life?

Every dumping has an additional tragic twist. Bittergirls around the world have confided that there are a few things they wish they'd had in place the night they got dumped.

"Cab fare! He was taking me out for dinner, so I came out with only my evening bag and no money—just contraceptives. Isn't THAT ironic?"

"Waterproof mascara—why the hell wasn't I wearing waterproof mascara?"

"Another stiff drink. No waiter would come near us once it started—suddenly I was a leper—they all knew. I desperately needed another Scotch. . . ."

"Now as soon as I get to a restaurant I always scan the room for the nearest exit—I thought I was making a beautiful, dignified departure and ended up in the cloakroom. . . . I had to turn around and do the whole thing over again. It kind of spoiled the effect."

In the split second it took Him to utter "I love you, I'm just not *in* love with you," your life has become like a carnival: the midway, the freak show, the funhouse all rolled into one with that off-key calliope soundtrack playing in your head. Sweetheart, you've been initiated. Welcome to the club.

Here's the reality. One way or another, He left.

Maybe you knew this was coming. No more wondering if everything is all right. No more walking on eggshells trying to make it work. No more waking up and asking yourself if this is the day He's leaving. Or maybe you've been blindsided by a Mack truck. You had no idea, no clue. Whatever the case, chances are you're still breathing. Okay, maybe that breath is a little ragged and maybe your chest aches from the sobbing, but here you are with no place to go but up. Honestly. There may be a few detours along the way, but up is your final destination. You've got the bittergirls with you.

For a bittergirl in the aftermath of a breakup, no reaction or action is out of bounds. We're here to tell you that whatever you're feeling, it's okay, honey. The bittergirls have been there, and we're here to share. At least now it's done. At least that moment is never going to happen again. Remember the movie *Groundhog Day*? Well, unless you insist on reliving The Incident, it's done; it's over. You'll never be in that place at that moment on that day with that guy ever again.

We, the original bittergirls, have been ditched in restaurants, on sailboats, in bed, at weddings, during therapy sessions, on airplanes, and at funerals. Collectively we've been dumped fifty-seven times. Does that make us losers? No. It makes us qualified to write this book.

The Pity Party

Getting dumped is painful, ugly, and lonely. It turns bright, articulate women into sobbing, snot-covered, mascara-streaming wrecks. It makes even the most fabulous woman question herself. "Maybe if my face was oval He wouldn't have dumped me." Getting dumped turns you inside out. You used to discuss world politics on national television; now you can barely rerecord your answering machine message without falling apart. You ran marathons; you ran with the wolves—and now you can barely get out of bed. What you feel is yours. Your feelings are facts. They're the only truth you know right now.

Everyone has been dumped. No ifs, ands, or buts. Whether you're reeling from Arthur leaving you with two toddlers and a mortgage or from when little Johnny took off across the playground with your best friend Audrey in second grade, getting dumped sets in motion a torrent of unpredictable behaviors.

Getting dumped becomes a daily physical struggle.

No matter how much sleep you get, you're still tired. No matter how much you eat, you're never full. Or you go days without eating and you're still not hungry. You fall asleep crying and you wake up crying. A day feels like a year. It's an uphill battle just to fill the hours. Stretches of time lie before you like never-ending roads surfaced with splintered glass that you must walk down. Oops! Watch your pedicure!

You feel like you're cracking and breaking into fragments of yourself and no one even notices. Worse still, the whole world is going on around you as if nothing has happened. HOW CAN THEY NOT KNOW? Your parents are still bickering about the noise the dishwasher makes, your cabdriver is bemoaning the shape of the economy. You don't care about the state of the world. How can you when your personal universe has been shattered? Your boss asks you to finish that report, your neighbors invite you to their housewarming party, your doctor tells you to increase your vitamin intake, your mechanic tells you to have a nice day—and all you want to do is scream, "What the hell are you talking about? Can't you see my world is falling apart?"

You pray for sleep so that you can stop thinking about how you're going to get through the day. You dream of Him and reach for Him, waking up, only to realize you're the only one in the bed.

You're walking to meet your friends for brunch and it starts to rain. The rainy Sunday conjures up images of Him and rumpled sheets, and suddenly you have to stop and gasp for air. You try to keep walking but it feels as though the wind has been knocked out of you and your legs are made of lead. You lean against a lamppost for support as you try to put one foot in front of the other. You never knew you could be weighed down by so much sadness. The sheer exhaustion of carrying the burden of losing Him is more than you can bear some days. Missing Him is like homesickness in your very own living room. The feeling of anger and rejection is replaced by weariness. You feel crippled by grief.

Every action feels false as you try to get through the day. There's a thin veneer over everything you do. Your face feels like it's going to split from all the fake smiles you've pasted on. You're an imposter in this new life. You want your old life back. You stare in open curiosity at your family, your friends, strangers on the street, wondering, "Who got my life?"

You leave the house simply to get away from the ghosts of your old life, but you feel haunted by your memories of Him wherever you are. You've looked into going to Ecuador to help build orphanages. But you blister in the sun. You're considering getting a cat. Honey, you're allergic.

Your center of gravity has changed and you can't seem to find your balance. Well, no wonder—you usually strut around in six-inch heels and now you're wearing a pair of ratty quilted slippers that Aunt Agnes left in your closet six Christmases ago. It's like the first trimester of pregnancy but without the joyful promise of new life—unending nausea, paralyzing fatigue, with your couch and remote control as your best friends. Pregnancy? You should be so lucky. Tears are streaming down your face as you're thinking, "What if nobody ever wants to have sex with me again?"

Please tell us you've replaced that godawful mascara with something waterproof.

Whether you were dating for five months, living together for four years, or married with three children, getting dumped means pain. Rejection is rejection, and whether you're a teenager or a grandmother, it stings. But as the bittergirls are here to tell you, what you do with that pain makes all the difference. The bittergirls say embrace the pain, embrace the bitterness. We are here to welcome you into the fold, regardless of how short, how long, or how harrowing your relationship may have been. As the bittergirl manifesto says, "We've all earned our scars." And these scars are your badges of honor.

Unsolicited Advice

There are books out there telling you what you did wrong, how to get Him back, how you can make the next man love you, how you can get married before thirty-five . . . no no no no no. The bittergirls know that you don't need to feel any worse than you already do. You don't need to be told there's something wrong with you. There's nothing wrong with you. You simply got dumped. Supermodels get dumped. Rock stars get dumped. Princesses get dumped. We're not here for relationship rescue. The only relationship that matters is the one you have with yourself.

There will always be well-meaning but clueless people on the periphery of your life who offer unsolicited advice. Some are going to tell you what you should do; some are going to tell you it's all for the best. What they *won't* tell you is what's going to be the hardest: no longer speaking in the Holy Trinity of "He and I," "Him and me," and "us." Knowing your plans for the weekend and that they consist of a rental movie and microwave popcorn. You've been going down one road together, and now you're alone and heading for a curve you can't see beyond. Lucky for you the bittergirls' limo has arrived, fully equipped with airbags and champagne.

asinine advice (that makes you want to kick them in the ass)

"Maybe you should have lied and said you didn't want kids either."

"Well, you need to let Him know His needs come first."

"I booked the reception hall. It worked. A week later He popped the question."

"You know what I did? I told Him I wanted a baby before my twenty-eighth birthday."

"You have to visualize what you want."

"I grew my hair. It changed everything."

"On Saturdays *we* like to fondue with friends. You should try it."

"I quit my job and drive a Winnebago around the country to be with Him while He works."

"I signed Him up for a men's group."

"Have you thought about swinging?"

"I had a breast reduction."

We've got to tell you—some people are going to pity you.

punchlines (or, lines that make you want to punch someone)

"Hey you, where's the boy?"

"Wow, you look great . . . CONSIDERING."

"Oh, babe. . . ."

"How-are-you-I-heard-I'm-sooooo-sorry. You guys were so perfect together."

"So, what's His deal?"

"I mean I thought you guys were, like, it, you know?"

"He-has-no-idea-what-He's-losing-NOW-tell-me-everything."

"You guys were so great, what a couple! How tragic for you . . . what are you now, thirty?"

"I mean, if you two couldn't make it work, who can?"

"Just remember, everything happens for a reason."

Hold your head high and ignore these people. Lots of other people are going to be there for you. Especially the bittergirls.

Pop Went Your Kernel

Hey, it's not about Him leaving. That's not *all* this is about. It's about that part of you He took when He left. That Kernel. Knowing that He's walking around with your Kernel and doesn't even know it.

The bittergirls say, "Sweetie, reclaim your Kernel!"

After all, once upon a time in a land far far away, you did actually have a life before Him. Remember that? Remember the days when you could decide on Friday afternoon that you were going to head off to New England for a weekend of camping with your girlfriends? When you could walk around the house singing Madonna songs in your fuzzy moosehead slippers? When a candlelit bath, a glass of Merlot, and a good magazine was your idea of a perfect night? Remember when you could crawl through the door drunk at 4 A.M. and not worry about waking Him up? When you didn't have to sneak into the house and hide your shopping bags before He realized you were home? Remember when you didn't have to get your colorist to write receipts for house paint?

All these things may be a distant memory, but they're elements of your past; they're in your DNA. And although right now you feel like your entire genetic makeup is about the breakup, it is *not*, and the bittergirls are here to remind you of that. Think about it. You've survived a lot of things in your life—and you're going to survive this too. Maybe you won't get over it right away. But in order to get over it, you're going to have to get used to it.

things you've survived

1. Wearing white pants the first day you got your period
2. Your first shaving gash
3. Tucking your skirt into your nylons before that job interview

4. Your father catching you having sex on the living room floor with your twelfth-grade boyfriend

5. Breaking someone else's heart

6. Puking all over yourself at a university frat party

7. Bouncing your first rent check

8. Telling your parents your best friend smashed up their new car

9. Your parents' divorce

10. Getting picked last for every sports team

11. Having to ask your parents for a loan after your third career in five years didn't work out

12. Reading a close friend's eulogy

13. Running out of gas in a snowstorm on the highway

14. Paying for condoms at the pharmacy as your boyfriend's mother steps into line behind you

15. Getting overlooked for that promotion and learning your assistant got it

16. Being betrayed by a friend

17. Realizing that you e-mailed your first attempt at poetry to All instead of Al in your address book

18. The time you went into anaphylactic shock at a concert and the show was stopped so the paramedics could get to you in the floor seats

19. Dyeing your hair one color and it coming out another, the night before the prom

20. Realizing (at the reception) the dress you're wearing to your sister's wedding is see-through

Now, we could tell you that you'll get through this breakup easily and without pain. We could tell you that we'll help you get Him back, and that there's a handy-dandy solution to all your problems. We could promise that you'll never feel hurt like this again. But the reality is that the only way to prevent yourself from feeling anything else from this point onward is to live under a rock. And what kind of life is that?

So What's a Girl to Do?

Why, become a bittergirl, of course! And what is a bittergirl you might ask?

In the trenches of heartbreak hell lie many a fledgling bittergirl. We're here to help pick you up, pull out the shrapnel, straighten your uniform, and send you back into the world with guerrilla tactics, unstoppable strength, and impenetrable self-esteem.

A bittergirl learns to turn her life around on her own terms and take on the world again with a sense of humor, a sassy attitude, and a team of gals by her side. She is cheeky yet glamorous in her own unique way, and plays an integral part in our society.

Bittergirls are everywhere. You'll see one in a neighborhood bistro as she laughs heartily with her circle of friends. You'll exchange a meaningful glance with one at the hardware store as you choose a new setting for your power drill. Even the cashier at the grocery store will squeeze your hand knowingly as she gives you back your change.

This underground movement has even infiltrated top levels of government. It controls our banks and corporate infrastructure. It has spread its limbs worldwide through the arts, health organizations, education systems, charities, export markets, medical fields, farming, tourism, scientific research, and the NHL.

Whether you're sixteen or ninety-three, whether you're married, divorced, single, or cohabiting, dating seriously or seriously parenting, a grandmother or a granddaughter, once you're a bittergirl you're always a bittergirl.

And as any bittergirl can attest, bittergirls are bettergirls.

Wouldn't You Like to Be a Bittergirl Too?

Joining the bittergirls doesn't mean building a clubhouse, dancing around a magic toadstool, or sending away for a secret decoder ring. It means opening yourself up to the possibility that things will get better, that life will go on, that you will not let yourself be defined by this breakup. First of all, this is not about blame. It's not about blaming yourself, Him, or anyone else involved. Being a bittergirl is not about getting over Him so you can be with someone else.

A bittergirl soon discovers that she can be sad and wallow in self-pity for a while. She can be angry and vengeful for a bit, she can be malicious and spiteful and a pain in the ass, but when all is said and done, she's the one who has to move on and up. And she will.

Becoming a bittergirl is an evolutionary process. You don't just wake up one morning, evening gown on, tiara in place, martini in hand, and announce to the world that you're a bittergirl. There are rites of passage you must go through. Then one day you'll wake up and it won't matter what you're wearing, you will just be. A bittergirl. Later, you might stop for a split second with that feeling like you've checked out of your hotel room and left something behind. And then it will hit you: You have absolutely everything you need. You might be standing at a cocktail party looking and feeling glamorous and you'll be relaying your breakup story as you flip your hair over your shoulder. People will laugh as you spin your yarn: "And then He. . . ."

Believe it or not, there will be humor in this heartache and there is a light at the end of the tunnel. So wipe those eyes, push the hair out of your face, take a good look in the mirror, and visualize the most fabulous life you could possibly imagine. Save that snapshot for your memory bank. You're creating your own Declaration of Independence. You're about to take your first step on the bittergirl journey, and it's going to be the ride of your life.

🍸 bitteractivity

Gently Does It   Let's take it gently for the first chapter. Your exercise for today is to get up, blow your nose, wash your face, and brush your teeth.

two

pick a dump, any dump

WHAT WAS HE LIKE? How would you describe His face, His clothes, His voice? No, we're not talking about the man He was when you were together. We're talking about the venomous, devious, low-down, pathetic excuse for a snake He was on the day He dumped you.

We dare you to share the pain. Double-dare you to share the horror stories. The bittergirls have witnessed it all, honey: breakups that will leave your mouth agape, breakups that will twist your already tenuous little heart into knots, breakups that will make you cringe in disbelief. There ain't nothing we haven't seen.

The Bittergirl Institute for Advanced Research on Dumping has amassed bundles of dastardly dumps that have been committed against us and our entourage of fledgling bittergirls. It has ascertained that, sadly, there are a number of time-honored styles of dreadful dumpings universally practiced on unsuspecting dumpees around the world. Take a gander at these wily ways and see if any strike a gong of recognition in what's left of your heart. Who would commit these heinous crimes on innocent bittergirls worldwide, you ask? Well, let's meet those nasty boys, often referred to as The Perpetrators.

The Coward

So, you've had the conversation. He's not happy, He can't exactly say why. He still loves you; He just needs to figure out some stuff. For months you've tried to talk. For months you've asked if anything's wrong and He's assured you that everything's fine.

You've had the conversation in bed, on your living room floor, in the car on the way home from your sister's wedding, as you were making a cake for His mother's sixtieth birthday. For months you've walked on eggshells, fearful of doing anything to upset His equilibrium. You've done everything physically possible to make His life happier, easier. You tackled the cleaning, you got a promotion at work so He wouldn't have to worry about the finances, you worked out twice a day so you could look good for Him. You were His rock, His bastion through these terrible, terrible times.

Then one day He admits He's looked at all the other areas of His life that could be making Him unhappy and that they're all fine. Maybe it *is* you. Your mannerisms, your being, your essence. But He admires you so much. You're so strong. Yet He still can't make the break. He suggests taking it one day at a time.

And this is where you, in your quest to make life easy for Him, are forced to step in and do the dirty work. You have to break up with yourself.

Meet THE COWARD.

The Coward. What is the allure of The Coward? You want to hate Him, you try and you try, but you just can't. When you close your tear-stained eyes, all you can do is see His handsome face looking back at you so longingly, His eyes so full of pain and love for you. He wishes this wasn't happening; He wishes He was the one staying. This is the hardest thing He's ever done. More longing looks.

The Coward wants to be liked. The Coward thinks He's a gentleman. The Coward thinks not talking about His feelings makes Him stronger, more dignified. So you turn into a screaming banshee trying to get an emotion out of Him while He e-mails you an alphabetized list of what's yours and what's His.

He packs His stuff with a heavy heart and weary shoulders. With each book He takes off the shelf or CD He puts in a box, He sighs. Is that a tear? He just knows He's going to be the bad guy in all of this. You feel so awful for Him that YOU help HIM pack. You even help Him move. "You are so strong," He says as He walks out the door. And voilà! You just broke up with yourself.

You'll feel the effects of The Coward years after He's out of your life if you're not careful. This is the long slow dump that plucks your heartstrings out one horsehair at a time. It is the dump that keeps on dumping.

When people hear about your breakup, they are shocked. "But you guys were so perfect together!" Now not only have you dumped yourself, you're the official spokesperson of the breakup. The Coward is simply charming when meeting the same people. You've already done all the work.

As The Coward begins His new life—staying at His parents' place, letting His hair grow, quitting the firm, or getting His '80s band back together—you're left in the aftermath. In your attempts to make it work, you turned into superwoman, you worked twice as hard, slept half as much, tried to live a life full enough for the both of you. Now that months of trying are over and you've broken up with yourself, you can finally stop and take a breath.

Be careful—here's where His powers are the deadliest.

Because He never actually dumped you, because He never said exactly what was wrong, because He made it all so seamless (right down to that alphabetized list of what's yours and what's His), you're left with the questions. "What if we *had* taken that trip to India?" "What if I *hadn't* cut my hair?" You'll spend sleepless night plagued with doubts: "I should have worked harder. I shouldn't have been the one to say it. Maybe He thinks I didn't love Him enough to fight harder." You'll blame yourself because, let's face it, you've done all the work so far, you might as well beat yourself up about it too. "It's because I couldn't ski, speak French, stop biting my nails, have an orgasm quickly enough."

He will follow you into your next relationship if you let Him. He will hover around like a ghost. He left you without a decent explanation, why shouldn't the new guy? The ghost of The Coward is deadlier than the actual man. When you bump into Him at a party He'll greet you like a long-lost friend, maybe even suggest lunch. He bears no scars because He just shed you like an old skin, while you've walked around carrying all His layers of angst and apathy.

The good thing about The Coward is that He's too afraid to incite change, so while you move on with your life He'll still be the same shadow of a man searching for something He had in the first place. He'll probably get drunk with His best friend a year from now and confess that He made the biggest mistake of His life. . . . Awww, is that a tear?

Magic Man

You're on your way back from your Wednesday night pottery class. He seems deeply moved by the harmony sculpture He's made, and you're admiring the matching clay bowls He helped you hand-sculpt. You imagine them sitting perfectly in the open-faced cabinets of the dream kitchen you'll build with Him. Of course, He'll design it. He is so creative! As you walk home along the lake, the water glowing in the soft moonlight, your heart fills with pride at the joy of being on the arm of this artist, this overflowing creative power.

He stops and looks soulfully into your eyes. The force of His gaze makes your knees wobbly. You're reminded once again of the passion of your first kiss. You lean in to bask in the warmth of His lips when He says "I can't do this." But He's so good at pottery, you tell Him. Just because He doesn't like this sculpture, He can make another one next week. "No. This. You. Me. I don't feel inspired anymore. I've lost my magic." You can't say anything. You are stunned. You tell Him you'll help Him find His magic. Maybe He left it on the pottery wheel? You'll do anything. But His eyes are already searching somewhere else, far, far away, somewhere you just can't quite reach no matter how hard you try.

Meet MAGIC MAN.

Ah, the charm of Magic Man. He saw you across a crowded room at His friend's art exhibit and claimed you as His own. He devoured you with His gaze. A cloud of enchantment hovered over you, and for a time you were His project, His painting, His sonnet. Ah, to bask in the light of such a talent. Then, just as His writer's block got the best of Him, suddenly He needed to be inspired again. Inspired *again*? Didn't you inspire Him? Wasn't your relationship full of music and laughter and light? Didn't He tell you you were a Botticelli painting with smaller hips? You are numb. Suddenly your poetic prose is gone and all you can do is say "Why, why, why . . . ?" He can't hear you, of course, because He's off in search of His next muse, His next hit, His next obsession.

"Don't fall in love with a dreamer, He'll only break your heart." Haven't you heard those words somewhere before? My God, your life has just gone from a Renaissance painting to a country song.

Magic Man needs to be inspired constantly. If His creative juices aren't flowing from your relationship, He'll go to the next fresh juice bar on the block. And while He's there, He'll probably need to borrow a couple of bucks. You see, He's always just a little bit broke. It's something He's working through with His shrink. He doesn't mean to hurt you; in fact, He still cares about you passionately, but without His muse He is nothing. Unfortunately, the muse who was once housed in your body took a leave of absence or skipped town, and you can't do anything about it.

He sucked up all your creativity, energy, and savings in His quest for His next big artistic endeavor. Without even realizing it you emptied your soul into His dreams, but it just wasn't enough to keep Him inspired. He's left you empty.

Ah, Magic Man, the enfant terrible of breakups. Magic Man's light is a hard one to extinguish. Nobody's attention will be quite the same for a while. But remember, girls, you want a relationship with a man, not a piranha.

Man Solo

You've just returned from teaching English in Korea together, or you were volunteers at a rain forest preservation group in Costa Rica, or maybe you met at a board meeting and never even left the city limits. But at some point in your adventure together, He got a faraway look in His eyes and said something vague about the call of the West, the urge to scuba dive off the Great Barrier Reef, or the need to reconnect with the child you never even knew He had. And faster than you can say "Send me a postcard," He's vanished. Gone. The only thing left of Him is His hemp choker and an empty bottle of patchouli oil. There were no nasty words, no ugly fights. He simply had to go; it's His nature. You couldn't have stopped Indiana Jones; how could you stop Him?

You'll never forget the night you met. He enthralled you with the story of how He tamed a wild stallion in Montana, how He built His solar-paneled cabin in the woods by Himself, how He learned French by living among the people in West Africa for a year. By the time He stroked your face with His calloused fingers you were putty in His hands. Suddenly your world burst into Technicolor as He cooked you exotic meals, taught you to tango, and recited passages from Anaïs Nin as He henna-tattooed your inner thigh. So what made Him go? Were you not adventurous enough? Couldn't eat spicy food? Didn't your stories about your all-girls summer camp compare with His pilgrimage across the Pyrenees? He seemed so into you.

Meet MAN SOLO.

Oh, the pull of Man Solo. The biting irony of Man Solo is that the traits that drew you to Him in the first place are the ones that destroyed you in the end. He mesmerized you with His stories of how He trekked through the Himalayas alone, he took a monthlong vow of silence at a Buddhist retreat, and rode His motorcycle through the Rockies. As He told these unbelievable stories, He lavished you with attention. When walking along the beach at sunset or waking up after a night of tantric lovemaking, He gave you that lazy smile and said, "I'm having a moment." You took it to mean a moment about you. No, honey, with Solo, it's never about you. His moments are His own. He lives for Himself and Himself alone.

In Man Solo's world, there are no ramifications. You were supposed to have a romantic dinner at your place. You spent the day cooking fresh lobster. He never showed up. He met a homeless bongo player at the pier, jammed with him, and then took him to a soup kitchen. How could you hate Him for that? HE'S SO THOUGHTFUL.

When Man Solo looks into your eyes, He's not seeing your future, He's seeing His own reflection. Man Solo is intense. He's hearing every word you say. He's there. But when He's not, you aren't even in His thoughts. He's finessed the art of detachment to perfection.

When He says goodbye He means it. That's not to say you'll

never see Him again. If you do bump into Him, Man Solo will probably remember you as one of His great love stories. He'll probably retell the story as though *He* were the victim and *you* broke His heart. The story will focus on Him as the leading man and all the good times you had. It will be so far from what you remember you'll wonder if He's actually talking about your relationship. Or He'll show up on your doorstep in five or six years because He was hiking in Thailand and the color of a flower reminded Him of your hair. He had a moment.

Teflon Man

You're sitting together in His car, in your home office, or in the boardroom at His work. He's been toiling away, busy building His career, and you've been so supportive. Your career is blossoming too, but you manage to balance it all: work, cleaning, cooking, staying fit, and, most of all, cultivating a successful relationship. His career is on the up and up. He's driven, ambitious, and focused: all things that you love about Him.

The car is in park, the emergency brake on. The fax machine is whirring, spitting out pages of that important report. The boardroom echoes with the sound of His voice as He says, "I can't explain. It's just a feeling I have." Dumbfounded, you say, "Explain the feeling."

He perks up as though a lightbulb just exploded in His head. "I've lost my drive, my passion. I can't love you AND my work too. It's draining me."

Stunned for a minute, you can't say anything. It's incomprehensible. That's not a reason. You won't let Him do this. "No. Tell me you don't love me anymore, you don't find me attractive anymore, that I'm nothing like the person you want to be with. Something I can grasp on to!"

Then, as if He's just closed a deal, His script has been sold, His quarterly report is out, He offers to drop you off at home, take you to your best friend's, or go to a hotel for the night.

You've been dumped. For absolutely unintelligible reasons. The only thing you can say is "Why?" as you plummet from contentment to misery in the time it takes Him to power up His BlackBerry.

Or maybe you're out for dinner. It's just you and Him in your favorite Saturday night restaurant. The lighting is low, the food is succulent, the red wine warms your palate. Or you're out for a long walk. You've been enjoying the silence, soaking up the sun, and basking in the warmth of His hand in yours. Children are laughing and playing around you, and you imagine one of them is yours.

He looks at you across the table/on the bench/wherever the hell you are. His eyes gloss over, He gets a pained look, and the free fall starts. "I don't know how to do this. It's too much, it's too soon, I feel trapped. . . ." The words tumble out and you cling to your seat, to your bench, digging your nails into the palm of your hand.

Sobs well up inside you. Your hands are trembling. He asks if you're all right. You attempt a broad smile through quivering lips. "I'm fine." He sees that you are not. Your mascara is running, people are staring. You gulp back your wine or look into the sun to blind yourself from crying. He gets up to leave, not wanting to make more of a scene, and you scream, "NO, DON'T GO, DON'T LEAVE ME!" But He's already gone. He doesn't stop to take care of the bill or to find out if you have enough money to get home. You're left with the check, the lint in your pockets, and your heart in your hands, in public, onstage. Twenty strangers have seen it all. Whoops, you've just slid off the edge of His life: no nasty messes for our Teflon hero to clean up here.

Meet TEFLON MAN.

He has an aura, a glow about Him. He's driven, He's successful, He wants only the best in life, and that apparently included you. He so admired how you handled it all, how it all came together in your capable hands.

But Teflon likes to admire such things from afar. He's an observer: He likes to surround Himself with beautiful things, but also likes the freedom to make His exit when and how He wants. He is the classic gourmand in the restaurant of life: He wants fine food and is willing to pay for the privilege, but He doesn't want to be stuck with the dishes. Teflon's self-worth comes from other people's opinions about Him. He needs to be the best at what He does, living for glowing reviews, high scores, good returns, and other people's envy. He is happiest when other people want to be Him, and He doesn't like to be alone, needing other people around to fuel His drive. You were just the high-achieving, fabulous companion He needed. He needed you to boost Him up, challenge Him, and be great in bed. He is a consumer. He sucked you up whole in His quest for His next big thing. But when you look like you might be as successful as Him at handling the whole enchilada, He drops you faster than Martha Stewart dumps stock.

Teflon Man can't be content at home and a shark in the boardroom too. You're simply another sacrifice He's made for the love of His game. And by the time you realize what's happening, reaching out and asking why, He's gone. And if the next day you looked in His BlackBerry, you'd find that your name, your number, and all your future engagements together were gone—delete delete delete.

The Mountie

He's been away on business, doing research, or on a golf trip with the buddies and now He's back. You've had a quiet family dinner in your newly renovated home; He's spent time with the kids and tucked them in. You're in bed. You're touching Him, just touching Him, and suddenly He stiffens, just stiffens, and says, "I have to go."

Where? To the kitchen, the bathroom? Go eat, go pee, go to France? Where? "I want to be a Mountie." He wants to be a Mountie. He's a forty-year-old asthmatic professor who hates guns. You ask, "Where did this come from?" "From me. From you not supporting me in my choices, in my— Do you think I just dreamed this up?"

Your mind is spinning. You coddle Him and tell Him you'll support Him: in His choices, in all that He wants to do. A career change at this point in your marriage, your life, seems strange but you'll work through it. You'll do whatever He needs.

"I don't know who I am anymore. This life, the children are crushing me. I need to be alone, just myself."

He dumps you and goes off in search of His space, in search of Himself. You're left with the children and the mortgage payments, weeping in the shower as the soap melts in your hands, wondering, "How did I get here?"

Meet THE MOUNTIE.

The Mountie. The man formerly known as your husband, your partner, your boyfriend. Anyone other than this stranger telling you He wants out. You look at His face, searching for clues of recognition. Is He in there somewhere? This is the same person you woke up with this morning, isn't it? You look into His eyes for some spark. But nothing's there, just this shadow of the man you love telling you, in an unfamiliar voice, that you are squeezing the lifeblood way the hell out of Him.

Oh yeah, He wanted the wife, the house, the kids, the whole nine yards, but oops! He's changed His mind. Now He wants to be a cop, a zookeeper, a CNN news anchor—anything other than the man who shares your bed and the bills.

The Mountie is less lethal than The Coward and not as charming as Magic Man. He is fumbling and lost but still difficult to get over. His sudden declaration of misery is so shocking it sends you into a tailspin, questioning your entire life together up until that point.

The Mountie is a man in crisis. It doesn't have to be midlife; it just has to be life changing. The Mountie has never fully understood the "when the going gets tough" philosophy. He is in search of a quick fix. He quickly blurts out His unhappiness, quickly creates a new life, and quickly forgets you were ever a part of it. You, meanwhile, are still dumbfounded, rooted to that same spot in the kitchen. It all happened so fast. While you're reeling, He's getting His motorcycle license.

The Mountie has left you knee-deep in the middle of a life you created together. Now He's on a plane to Belize to photograph nature and you've got to figure out how to transfer the car insurance and get your child to school by nine.

You know The Mountie's unhappiness comes from within; however, to The Mountie it's all your fault. Your life together is confining Him. "I feel trapped. I need to be alone. Anywhere. Anywhere but here. You're crushing me. I can't count on you for support." Your pleas to make it work have fallen on deaf ears. He is out the door.

Missing in Action Man

Everything seems to be going along fine. He's met your friends and you've met some of His. Your family has approved and your brother actually calls Him by His name. You stay over at each other's places on weekends because it's too complicated during the week. He has a toothbrush at your apartment and you've befriended His roommates. Sometimes when you're lying in bed it seems like His thoughts are in another world. He doesn't always call when He says he will, and you're not always sure where He is, but that's all part of the mystery and intrigue that keeps you interested. You have a romantic date planned for Saturday night. This scenario plays out one of two ways.

1. It's Thursday. You get in from after-work cocktails with the office gals and you go to check your phone messages. There's a message from Him. "Listen, I'm so sorry to have to do this. I know you're out right now, but I've decided to go away for the weekend, so I'm leaving early in the morning. Look, this just isn't working out. I think you're great, I'm just not ready for anything serious. I'm not in a place where I can give much to a relationship right now. Take care. I'll talk to you soon. I'm sorry." You press replay on your phone and double-check that this message is from Him, coming from His phone number.

2. It's Saturday. You haven't talked to Him since Thursday when He said He'd call you Saturday afternoon. He hasn't returned your four messages. You sit in your living room in your short strappy black dress picked out especially for this occasion. At midnight you're still sitting in your dress, wrapped in an afghan with a now-empty pizza box on the coffee table alongside a drained bottle of Chardonnay, watching reruns of *The Love Boat*, waiting for His call. A little wobbly, you decide to make your way to the fridge. Just one more glass of wine wouldn't hurt. You are stuck in time. Has His sister been diagnosed with terminal cancer, is His ex-girlfriend pregnant, did His dog die, is He secretly married, is He gay? You sit by the phone, His toothbrush in your hand, waiting for Him to call.

Meet MISSING IN ACTION MAN.

Ah, the thrill of MIA Man. MIA Man is like a spy; He's a man of mystery. He's the James Bond of the breakup. He's handsome, interesting, and just slightly out of reach. One minute He loves you, the next He's tied up with Pussy Galore. You'll probably never hear about Pussy or His next international mission because He dumped you by e-mail or over the phone. In some cases you just never heard from Him again after He kissed you goodnight at your door. When He said "I'll call you Saturday," He meant some Saturday in 2020. Bastard.

MIA Man does not like emotional conflict. He will go to any length to avoid confrontation; hence the "faceless" dump. His motives are premeditated. He knew it was coming and He knew how it was going to be executed. You, on the other hand, are the unsuspecting victim who must move on with the knowledge that you will never see Him again. Nor will you ever really know why your relationship wasn't successful.

Don't ask why and don't try to find Him. Someday you may read about Him in the paper and say "I dated Him," but you probably can't prove it unless you saved His farewell message. Besides, it was all so fleeting and He had so many important matters to attend to.

Trigger

You're at Brian and Kelly's wedding, your cousin's bar mitzvah, His office Christmas party, your brother's convocation. You're surrounded by family and friends. The atmosphere is charged with goodwill, with love, with emotional connections. Laughter abounds, embarrassing stories are shared, speeches recited. You dance, you cry with joy, you fall down laughing when Uncle Joe sings "I Am, I Said" on karaoke. Whatever the occasion, it's enough to trigger a reaction from Him that's so out of left field it will leave you reeling.

As you make your way back to the hotel room, He says, "There's too much love. I can't do this. I can't give you what you need. You deserve so much more than me." The celebration has made Him realize: His family isn't as close as yours, He's not Jewish, He can't live up to your expectations, your mother will never approve, He has skeletons in His closet, He picked His nose when He was three, He has issues.

You try to convince Him that none of these things matter if you truly love each other. He says He doesn't think His love will ever be enough for you. He sees the love you need, the way you can flourish.

He takes care of the hotel bill and you are left, by yourself, downing the vodka and M&Ms from the minibar with the duvet pulled up to your chin in the king-sized massage bed, angry at your parents, your friends, His sister, His office for making Him feel like He wasn't good enough.

Meet TRIGGER.

Trigger. Oh, the deceptive charisma of Trigger. He might be forty, he might be twenty-five. He looks like a grown-up on the outside, but on the inside He's just a big baby, a well of insecurities. How were you to know? He wears His disguise well.

Trigger is the ultimate closet pessimist. He's the kind of guy who'll never run for the bus. What's the use? He'll just miss it anyway. He hates cutting the grass. It's just going to grow back. What you think is laissez-faire is a cover for something deeper. Trigger probably wept the first time you made love. He called your brother "Champ" and traced your family tree for your dad's birthday. Oh, the hours you spent imagining Christmas cards with both your names signed on them. You daydreamed about you and Trigger and your kids playing tennis up at the cottage.

But you just couldn't have fathomed the depths of Trigger's deeply hidden insecurities. Try as you might, you won't ever understand His skewed perception that He will simply never be good enough for you.

While at your parents' for the weekend, nursing your broken heart, a letter arrives for *them* from Trigger explaining how He really hopes

He's not going to be the bad guy in all of this and maybe they can keep in touch. You tell them they can't.

In the time you spend wallowing over Trigger He'll be weeping over someone new, swelling with emotion over her chihuahua yet not feeling good enough for even the little pup's affection.

The Louse

There you are one evening, doing what you do, juggling schedules, dropping the kids at hockey practice and picking up the dog at the vet, your mind filled with nothing more than "If I get to the grocery store on the way home I can pick up something fast for dinner, but if I order pizza I'll be able to get my suit from the dry cleaner so I'll have it for that board meeting tomorrow" when your cell phone rings. It's your best friend. She tells you to open up the paper to page thirteen's social column, and there is the picture of your husband with His arm around some woman. She's young and blonde and very pretty, not wearing much clothing to speak of, and they're at some bar? What? The article is about how to pick up available men? Available? But wasn't He out at poker night last Friday?

Or: It's a man, a voice you've never heard before, and he's crying, he's sobbing, he's asking you to please do something about the situation— what situation? "Your husband is ruining my marriage—please tell Him to stop the affair with my wife. . . ." His voice trails off into distraught weeping followed by a click and a dial tone.

Or: It's the travel agency; they want to confirm the trip to the Bahamas next week. For two. They couldn't get the honeymoon suite—would a deluxe room do? You're booked to take the kids to your parents' next week because your husband is flying to Pittsburgh to be the keynote speaker at the Roofing and Tile Manufacturers Convention.

This is the Nuclear Dump: the ballistic dump, the firestorm that leaves nothing in its wake. This is the man you have trusted, you have loved, you have raised a family with, the man you never doubted because you never had reason to. You met at university and He wooed you. You were different from the other girls, not superficial, not just fluff. He wanted you because you were real, and He would never leave you. He didn't flirt with other women, and if He did, it didn't mean anything, because He always said, "Why go out for sashimi when you can have sushi at home?" Well, honey, He's been sneaking out for that raw fish.

Meet THE LOUSE.

The Louse is legendary; The Louse is legion. Everyone has a story about either a Louse they knew and loved or a louse who dumped someone they love. The Louse was formerly the Greatest Guy on the Planet, the loving and loyal husband who could be trusted by all. Which of course is The Louse's biggest advantage in Lousedom: Who would suspect Him? He's such a great guy.

And apparently He's had you so wrapped around His mental little finger that you had no idea. Because to The Louse it's logical, it all makes sense. When He loved you, He loved you as much as He was capable of. It's just that you never asked Him to define His terms. Yes, He wanted to be with you always, but He wanted to be with some other women too. He never told you any lies. It was all true. True at that particular moment in time. He used that line about going out for sashimi—but you never asked Him if He liked to pick up sushi on His lunch hour. And He wanted a woman who was real, who had depth at home, but while He was at work, out of town, or out to dinner, He actually did want a little bit of arm candy.

There's no point in arguing with The Louse. He will not see the error of His ways. To Him, there wasn't one. The error in judgment in His eyes was yours, for not understanding that He has needs, and you just aren't filling them. He didn't do anything wrong; He certainly never meant to hurt you. Because it's all about Him, baby. He's just doing what He needs to do, and who are you to get in His way? The devotion that stood you in such good stead when He was with you is now turned in a different direction, and that direction is out the door.

The Revolving Door

You know Him. You've loved Him. He's loved you, then left you, then loved you and left you again. And again. And again. And again.

Your friends are at the point where they won't let you speak His name in their presence. You've exhausted their support and their sympathy. Every time you take Him back you promise them that "It'll be different this time," and every time He dumps you they're the first ones you call to come and pick up the pieces. They prop you up, dry your eyes, cancel your appointments for the day, making you promise not to take His calls. And you don't. Because He doesn't call for a day, a week, a month, a year.

Then one night you come home from the first really great night out where you never even mentioned His name, you danced to "I Will Survive," maybe you even flirted a little with someone new, and guess what? His spidey senses tingled and He realized you might be getting over Him. You might even see His name on your caller ID, but why not answer? It's okay. You're getting stronger and you wouldn't ever consider taking Him back. You Are Not A Doormat. Besides, your friends and family would disown you.

You pick up the phone.

He misses you. His voice is husky with emotion. What was He thinking? He's nothing without you. His world is empty. He just needed to figure that out. Now He knows. He really knows this time. You guys can't just throw all your history away. You two can't be with anyone else. It's you and He against the world. You're Bonnie. He's Clyde. Nobody understands what you guys have. Your friends are just jealous of the passion, the intensity you share. Can He come over?

And before you can say "Never again," He's back. His toothbrush hangs in its rightful place and His favorite coffee beans perch proudly on the counter. Your toilet seat is always up.

You keep Him a secret. You invent excuses why you can't meet your sister for dinner, you lie to your best friend about why you missed her birthday party. You don't go to your favorite brunch place with Him in case somebody spots you. You feel like you're cheating on the rest of your life. But you can't go public with Him until you're sure you guys are strong enough.

When you finally do break the news to your family and friends that you're happy, they don't seem surprised. Why would they? They've seen this pattern before. You need them, you cry on their shoulder, you talk incessantly about Him, you monopolize their lives with your heartbreak, then you drop off the face of the earth. And when you reemerge as if on schedule, it's with The Revolving Door on your arm. Why is it any different this time? You get defensive, you defend Him, this time it *is* different. Your friends are just judgmental. They don't understand.

And in the blink of an eye it happens again. You find the phone number in His pocket, He gets that faraway look in His eyes, He talks about becoming a paramedic in Afghanistan. And there you are. On the floor. In a ball. Reaching for the phone.

Meet THE REVOLVING DOOR.

Oh, the blissful monotony of The Revolving Door. His powers are a mystery. There's nothing particularly remarkable about Him. He doesn't invent new excuses, He doesn't try new tricks. Why would He when the old ones always work so well? He just loves you one minute and can't bear to be with you the next. Maybe it's His philandering ways, maybe He had a difficult relationship with farm animals, maybe He needs to be alone to compose His rhyming poems about fish—whatever. What is it about Him that turns otherwise strong, capable women into doormats? Doormats without any judgment?

He's not the most handsome, the funniest, or the smartest. He's just a guy with a commitment problem. He loves you, He loves you not . . . The Revolving Door will make you think your "On Again, Off Again" two-step is the stuff of great romance. It's not, sweetie. It's a broken record.

Your relationship with The Revolving Door could have ended years ago, but He calls out of the blue when His mother is sick and He "needs your strength," or He "needs to go back to the time when He was the happiest." He sucks the marrow right out of you while you get Him past whatever it is He's going through. Or, you live in San Francisco, He lives in Montreal. The Revolving Door doesn't want to live in the same city as you. He doesn't want to see you on Friday night. He just wants to call you at the end of the day to complain about His boss, talk about old times, maybe get together for a drink when His band is in town next. Hey, did you get that note He wrote you on a placemat from a diner in Duluth? Yeah, He was just thinking about the old days. You guys had some crazy times, huh? Then there's the night He was having a drink after work at the bar around the corner from your old place and He remembered it was your birthday last week. He's never missed your birthday by more than a month has He? Well He just thought He'd call, and, hey, can He come over? You let Him. You're strong now, how harmful can it be? Then in an instant He's gone again.

You think you can change Him. You can love Him enough to make up for any hurt or disappointment He's ever had. If you don't give up on Him then maybe He'll stop giving up on you. Honey, the second you stop letting Him in, taking His calls, and letting Him wipe His feet on you, He'll find someone else to revolve with. It's who He is. In His defense, The Revolving Door can only revolve if you let Him. He can show up at your door but you don't have to let Him in.

So you've met The Perpetrators. Now sugar, don't beat yourself up if you've known and loved more than a few of these dismal excuses for masculinity. Bittergirls are not about regret or living in the past. We are about getting over those soulless shits and moving on with what is to become an even more fabulous life. After all, if He told you He lost His magic, He was probably an imposter to begin with. Wants to be a Mountie? Does He realize that when He shoots the gun He's not the one making the "bang bang" sounds? Man Solo needs to be alone? Wow, what great sex He'll be having with Himself. But that isn't your concern because there are many dazzling adventures ahead on this bittergirl excursion. So hold on to your heart, breathe deep, and brace yourself for the next marvellous installment of your very own trip to bittergirldom. Line up. It's time for roll call.

bitteractivities

1. Rename That Man   You may feel that The Louse doesn't adequately describe Him. Maybe you want to call Him The Louse with the Flaxen Hair or Magic Man with the Little Wand. Get creative. Maybe you have a man that The Bittergirl Institute for Advanced Research on Dumping hasn't encountered yet. Describe Him in detail and send Him on over to us.

2. The Lost Weekend   Erase the day He dumped you from your calendar, datebook, planner . . . any visible schedule that you come across in your day-to-day routine. Cut it out entirely or paste in something you like to look at instead of the words "7 P.M. meet John Biffi's Bistro." Did you draw a miniature axe on the date in your little black book to symbolize The Incident? Cover it up with a sparkly sticker of a Gerber daisy that you lifted from your niece's sticker collection. Are there tear stains? Not to worry, the torso of February Man from the fireman calendar would look mighty good there. It's all part of the process of reclaiming your days.

3. The Punchline   This is where a bittergirl begins to laugh. No, really, it's possible. If you can bear it, go through the dumping in your head. Review every single sad, squalid second. What was the one detail that made your bestbittergirlfriend gasp in horror? Take that line and make it into an outrageous one-liner. No matter how agonizing it is to say it out loud, there's something shockingly funny in how He did it. It's in there. You can find it.

"He dumped me at the dinner table after meeting my parents."

"He said afterward, 'I hope we can still make love.'"

"As He was literally walking out on me and the kids, He turned to me and asked, 'Did you wash my soccer uniform?'"

4. Sweet Reward   Now, reward yourself with a chilled glass of Chardonnay or a warming glass of Merlot. Throw on a face mask and put some cucumbers or tea bags on those puffy eyes. Run a brush through that hair or at the very least sprinkle some baby powder at the roots. (It hides the grease for when the delivery boy comes.) Throw on some lip gloss and repeat to yourself: "I am fabulous" or "At least I'm not The Coward."

three

roll call

WE KNOW YOU'RE FABULOUS. We know you strive to listen intently in all your relationships. We know you can pick a little *schmatte* off a deep-discount sale rack at H&M and accessorize it to look like the latest hot designer creation. We've tasted those scrumptious meals you've whipped up at a moment's notice when it looked to us like the cupboards were bare. We've seen you fix the glitch that's been plaguing our computer. We've watched you calculate our tax return as we sobbed on your office recliner. We know what a complete package you are.

BUT, in the aftermath of The Incident, as you wallow in heartbreak hell, *who have you become?* Someone you've never seen before? At The Bittergirl Institute for Advanced Research on Dumping, we've seen them all.

Paralytic Girl

The moment He left, you headed straight under the covers, barely stopping to grab your bag of mini Mars bars. You tune out the world completely. You might as well have fallen off the edge of the earth (it would be preferable, of course). The curtains are drawn. You can't get out of bed no matter how hard you try. You won't answer the phone. You've called in sick every day for three weeks. They're beginning to wonder if you have a chronic illness. You tell them you do. It's called heartbreak.

There's a bottomless well somewhere inside you that's pumping fresh tears to your eyes at regular intervals. Just when you think you can't cry anymore, something else sets you off and another box of tissues meets a timely end.

Your pajamas smell rank but you no longer care about laundry. Your hair is so greasy you can put it into cornrows yourself. As long as you've got your remote control, your microwave, and a hotplate on your bedside table, you think you might just survive. There's a growing pile of empty popcorn bags and chocolate bar wrappers at the end of your bed. You used to be a gourmet chef. Now Kraft macaroni and cheese is your pièce de résistance. Between ordering *100 Love Songs* double discs and buying every infomercial product on the air, you've maxed out your credit cards. If you bothered to open your mail, you might even know that. The postman has started using your recycling bin for your letters because he can't cram any more bills through the mail slot.

You are spent. When He walked out that door He not only stole your heart, He took every ounce of your joie de vivre with Him.

👄 bittergirlspeak

Honey, we know. It's awful. You feel like you're plumbing the depths of your soul and there's not much to see. On a positive note, this is the lowest you will ever sink. It may seem like a monumental task, but just doing one thing a day to link yourself back to reality will work wonders. Whether it be allowing your bestbittergirlfriend to climb through your window and place a wet facecloth on your tear-streaked face or checking a single voicemail a day, one task at a time will reconnect you to the life outside your door.

Searching Girl

You're looking for help, for answers, for something to soothe your wounded soul. He couldn't respond when you asked Him why, so you're on a mission to find something, anything that will help you make sense of it all.

You've tried yoga, meditation, chi gong, and tai chi. You attended a silent retreat but all you wanted to do was scream. You've gone through twelve religions in a week. You've adapted part of the Hail Mary and repeat it as your mantra when you chant your prayers at night. "Hail Mary, full of grace, blessed are you among women. But do you know anything about men? Pray for me, now, at the hour of my heart's death. I swear I will sacrifice all my earthly burdens if only you will bring Him back to me again."

You've consulted a tarot card expert and had your palms read, your aura studied, your chakras balanced. Your handwriting analysis seems perfectly in tune with the tea leaf reading and numerology chart you had done.

You read His horoscope every day and compare it with yours, hoping your stars will align. You clip out His ascending and descending signs just to make sure you don't miss anything.

You've sent a questionnaire to His friends and family asking them what they think His definition of happiness is.

You've scoured mystical magazines and know about every spiritual-guidance course being offered within a hundred-mile radius. You've completed all the exercises in your self-help books that are supposed to cultivate peace in your heart. You don't go anywhere without your journal. You've tried black magic, prophetic affirmations, magic rocks, essential oils, and a new herbal remedy that's supposed to summon the spirits of loved ones.

He shattered your belief system entirely and you're scrambling to find something else to take its place. You believed in "Us," in "We," in "Him," and now you're left with nothing but questions.

👄 bittergirlspeak

This is a never-ending quest: the pursuit for some kind of answer here. As we'll often remind you, there's never a clear answer to why this happened. But as Searching Girl, at least you're getting exposed to myriad spiritual customs and traditions, even if some of them may be a little far-fetched.

bittergirls throughout history

Hera, wife of Zeus

Queen Elizabeth I

Queen Elizabeth II

Mary, Queen of Scots

Anne Boleyn

Queen "Bloody" Mary I

Princess Diana

Cleopatra

Clytemnestra

Medea

Lizzie Borden

Dorothy Parker

Sylvia Plath

Maria Callas

Superbittergirl

Superbittergirl! You're the action hero of breakups. Nobody ever sees you weak. The minute He utters the words "It's not you, it's me," your drawbridge is raised and nobody is getting close to your lair. There will be no tears, no pathetic attempts to get Him back, no losing your dignity at any cost. From the minute the door closes on His sorry ass you swing into action. You take a deep breath, change the answering machine message, and begin what you think is the healing. Your immediate goal is to be better. At everything. Within days of getting dumped you land that huge account, get that part, win three cases in a row, and perform never-before-heard-of surgery.

You've redecorated the house, tackled that closet in the hallway, re-grouted the bathroom tile, cleaned out the junk drawer, and held a garage sale with the proceeds going to charity. In between chairing the board of your local conservation society, reading to the blind, and feeding the homeless, you're training for the Iron Man Triathlon. Your theme song becomes "I Am a Rock, I Am an Island." The picture of Him on your desk at work has been replaced by photos of Joan of Arc and Wonder Woman.

When people question the breakup (and they will, you two were just so perfect together!) you will hold their hand and reassure them that it's-all-for-the-best-you're-just-fine-there-is-just-so-much-to-accomplish-in-a-day-that-you-barely-have-time-to-breathe!

💋 bittergirlspeak

Oh, sweetheart, you're the prime candidate for a Bittergirl Breakdown. You'll continue at this breakneck speed, refusing to acknowledge your sadness and disappointment, until the day you shrink your favorite sweater in the wash, burn the toast, or stub your toe. Then your carefully constructed shield of armor will melt away faster than you can say "Bittergirl Powers Activate!" The quest to be better at everything doesn't take away the fact that He dumped you. At the end of the day you're still you, and you'll probably be exhausted from that damn triathlon. So give yourself a break and some much-needed time out.

Reasonable Girl

Also known as The Doormat. Reasonable Girl is Superbittergirl's close cousin. Most people look at you and say, "Wow, you are really handling this well—you're so reasonable!" You won't hear a word said against Him: He's having a hard time, He doesn't know what He wants, He just needs to figure some stuff out. It's not that you're making excuses for Him; you're probably absolutely telling the truth. He probably *is* having a hard time right now, suffering from male menopause or questioning His sexuality . . . but instead of being angry about how this has shattered your world, you are just infinitely, insufferably REASONABLE.

"It takes two to make a relationship," you, Ms. Reasonable, will say, "and it takes two to let it break down." "I'm just as much to blame," you'll say calmly as you deliver His belongings neatly packed to His new bachelor pad. People will ask how you're doing, and you'll smile and say, "Fine—better than Him, I think . . . have you seen Him lately? He doesn't look so good."

💋 bittergirlspeak

Reasonable Girl will eventually have a ballistic Bittergirl Breakdown. It might leak into different areas of her life: Suddenly she'll become the Road Rage Queen. She could go on a rampage at work firing people because she didn't like the way they glanced at her chart in the team meeting. She's tamping down the anger from her breakup and refusing to acknowledge the injustice she's feeling. It's got to spurt out somewhere, and you can bet your bottom dollar it's going to be big and it's going to be inappropriate.

celebrity bittergirls

Patsy Cline

Zelda Fitzgerald

Anjelica Huston

Debbie Reynolds

Cynthia Lennon

Loni Anderson

Mia Farrow

Ellen DeGeneres

Carly Simon

Ivana Trump

Nancy Sinatra

Minnie Driver

Sadie Frost

Roseanne Barr

Lisa "Left Eye" Lopez

Halle Berry

Elizabeth Hurley

Public Sobber

From the moment He dumped you, and it was probably a public dump, you haven't been able to hold back the floodgates. You weep at the sight of a couple kissing goodbye at the train station. You bawl at the song playing in the waiting room at your chiropractor's office. When they don't have that Steve Madden pump in a size 8. When you notice the first star at night. At *Bambi*.

In the middle of a presentation to your agency's biggest client you turn to the VP of Creative and say, "Could you just hold me for thirty seconds while I cry?" You start to preface things with "I'm probably going to cry when I tell you this. . . ." whether you're talking about the breakup, what the long-range weather forecast is, or what you got your sister-in-law for her birthday. There is no limit to your capacity for salty tears.

👄 bittergirlspeak

Pulling a Holly Hunter from *Broadcast News* is one thing, but Holly had the decency to draw the curtains, unplug the phone, and do it in private. Sure everybody cries, and some of us cry more than others. But there are limits. It's nice when someone holds your hand as you cry, but who can follow you around twenty-four hours a day? You never stop. It's one thing to cry in front of your best friend or your mother; it's quite another to cry in front of your bank manager. It's understandable that you burst into tears or get dewy-eyed at your cousin's wedding or the late-night showing of *Truly Madly Deeply*. But it's not appropriate to hijack your best friend's husband's fortieth birthday party or a Super Bowl celebration with your convulsive sobs. There are going to be times in this breakup when it's just not about you. And healthy though it may be to let some of your emotions out, there's a time and a place. You're feeling lousy already—you don't need the itchy bloodshot eyes, the blotchy skin, and the bright red nose. You can't wear dark sunglasses all day every day. They just don't look suitable at your pelvic exam or Junior's parent–teacher conference. If you feel the need for a public wail, book a massage or sign yourself up for primal scream group therapy, and let it all hang out.

Busy Busy Martyr

Does your datebook look something like this?

7:30 A.M.	Time to get up!
8 A.M.	Make lunch for school bag, breakfast for the child, coffee for you.
8:30 A.M.	Take the child to school.
9 A.M.	Rush to the gym.
11 A.M.	Run out of the Y, leap into car, and race to 11:15 meeting with the woman you need to get that contract from.
NOON	Drive back to the school—it's volunteer-in-the-library day!
2 P.M.	Home! Check messages, get dinner ready for the child and the sitter.
3 P.M.	Dress for work, rush out the door with a peanut butter bagel in hand.
3:30 P.M.	Work till 9 P.M.—Done.
9:30 P.M.	Home, pay off sitter, call her a cab.
10 P.M.	Pick up around house, do dinner dishes, check on child.
10:30 P.M.	Answer phone messages, do paperwork for tomorrow, check schedule, set up the child's knap-

sack for school, check her homework, set table for breakfast.

11 P.M.   Tuck the blue sweater you made Him into the fireplace, pour a little lighter fluid on it, set a match to it.

11:45 P.M.   Pour a stiff Scotch.

MIDNIGHT   Shower, cry.

12:30 A.M.   Soap has melted in your hand. Knock on the bathroom door: "Mommy, I need a drink of water."

12:35 A.M.   Tuck child back in, dripping wet, with towel falling off.

12:45 A.M.   Collapse on own bed.

7:30 A.M.   Wake up, stiff. Wet hair has dried in tangles. Drool crusted in corners of mouth. . . .

Sweetheart, darling, pet—has it occurred to you that you're turning into the Busy Busy Martyr? No time for any emotion, you have to get to that meeting on time. A spoke has fallen off one of your wheels but you can't stop to fix it. Busy Busy isn't on the same superhero mission as Superbittergirl. Busy Busy's quest is unselfish. She needs to make sure everyone around her isn't suffering any ill effects from her breakup. And while the bittergirls hate to generalize, Busy Busy is usually a mother. She needs to make sure the kids aren't just okay but flourishing. It's not enough to have dinner on the table every night; it must also include one of each of the five basic food groups *and* be the best meal they've ever tasted.

We know one Busy Busy who scheduled her recovery from her breakup into her daytimer for a weekend when the kids were off at Dad's. Busy Busy will put her dreams on hold to make sure everyone else's are realized. Busy Busy will move into Beyond Bitter if she's not careful. Or she'll paralyze everyone around her because they'll never be able to live up to her level of perfection. Or, once the kids leave her perfect house and head out into the world, she'll be left with nothing to focus on, because it's been all about the kids and never about her.

bittergirlspeak

Oh Busy Busy, put down that BlackBerry, that spatula, that schedule for Suzuki music classes. Deal with some of the anger and fear and disillusionment you're feeling. Don't go through this breakup as if it were a PowerPoint presentation. Sometimes the people around you don't need life to be perfect, they just need it to be explored. Just because He changed your ten-year plan doesn't mean you have to impose a new one on your kids. Let them join you on the journey. He's already taken your Kernel and possibly your faith in the future, but don't let Him take away the you that everyone knows and loves too. Nurture the dreams you've always had and don't schedule them out of your life. Then invite the bittergirls over for dinner—we hear you're the best cook around.

bittergirls in fiction

Miss Piggy

Thelma and Louise

Cathy from *Wuthering Heights*

Blanche DuBois from *A Streetcar Named Desire*

Amanda Wingfield from *The Glass Menagerie*

Glenn Close's character in *Fatal Attraction*

Norma Desmond from *Sunset Boulevard*

Joan Crawford in *Mildred Pierce*

The Evil Stepmother from *Snow White*
Selma and Patty Bouvier from *The Simpsons*
Lucy from *Charlie Brown*

Angry Girl

As soon as He dumped you, you became a ball of rage. Grr, you're angry at the world. You stand up and shake your fists at everything and everyone. Even the neighborhood bully would cower in fear if you crossed his path. Every time you think of Him you stoke the fire of your fury. But since you can't take it out on Him, you take it out on the tollbooth guy, your executive assistant, your accountant, your father.

You leave hateful messages on His answering machine threatening to sabotage His life. You order free diaper samples to be delivered to His office. You restart His Columbia House subscription and call His stockbroker to dump His high-end stocks. You refer to Him as The Fucker in casual conversation with such frequency that if someone overheard you they'd think you have Tourette's.

Your best friends are scared to call because anytime they try to reason with you, you bite their heads off. When a child throws a temper tantrum in line at the bank you shout at her mom to "Take a parenting course!"

The cashiers at the grocery store gently whisper the total of your produce bill so as not to outrage you. When the pizza delivery guy drops your order off, he buzzes your apartment, leaves the pizza inside the front door, and bolts for his car just in case the crust isn't as thin as you like it. You want someone to pay for your hurt and you'll be damned if you let down your anger guard for one moment. He caused this disaster and He wreaked this havoc on the world. It's His problem. He should have thought about the repercussions.

💋 bittergirlspeak

Oh, we've all called Him The Fucker and we've all raged against the world. Anger is indeed part of the healing process. You're not quite yourself right now, and this big ball of fury that has occupied your soul is breathing fire on a lot of people you love as well as all the innocent bystanders. Anger is good, but you might as well funnel it right into a success story.

Avoidance Girl

He dumped you yesterday and you've already moved out of town. You've taken a volunteer position to deliver food supplies in a Third World country. You jump at the chance to work on a cruise line that travels the Pacific Ocean. You dive into a new life as if it's the life you were meant to be living all along. Him? Him who? You make new friends, create new hobbies, immerse yourself in this fresh environment, conveniently erasing all connections to Him.

When people from your old life try to contact you, you avoid their calls. You stay away from any reminders of Him or the years you spent together. It's as if someone hacked into your brain and stole your memory chip of Him.

Since He left your life, you too want to run as far away from it as possible. If He can do it, why can't you?

💋 bittergirlspeak

If you're fleeing the country or even the city where The Incident happened, odds are you're in avoidance mode. We all need a little bit of avoidance, a bit of checking out of the world. But the reality of the situation will always come back to haunt you, whether it be next week or years from now. Eventually, because the world is so small, there will come a time when you won't be able to run away from yourself any longer. You'll realize how important your friends are, how comforting your home can be, and that the life you used to live has a lot of valuable things to offer (aside from Him, that is).

Slutty Girl

He left you at the restaurant table or on the park bench or sitting on the new chaise longue He bought you for Valentine's Day last year, and within five minutes (or maybe a day or two) you're at the same table, bench, or chaise longue with Jacques, the dishy waiter, making eyes and getting frisky. Jacques satisfies you for a while but then you get distracted by Smoky Jim, the mysterious musician who plays folk music at your brother's pub. Smoky Jim is a whirlwind in bed, but when he has to go on tour you're not too bothered because Theo, the graphic designer you worked with last month, is taking you out on Friday night. Theo turns out to be a hopeless romantic. He wines you and dines you and doesn't seem to mind that you're being wooed by his pal, Jonni (yes, with an *i*). Jonni is a bit of the jealous type, though, so you decide it's best not to see either of them again. Ah, alone for a minute? No, Piero is on his way over to take you to the golf club for a dinner overlooking the eighteenth green.

Your best friend calls to see if you're okay. "Okay with what?" you say.

👄 bittergirlspeak

Kinda like Avoidance Girl, this one will catch up with you eventually. Maybe one day Piero will call and cancel and the entire sordid history of you and The Ex will hit you like a twenty-car pileup. Sometimes, just sometimes, it's good to take a moment, look at the situation, and deal with it before you head off into uncharted territory.

Substitution Girl

In whatever way with whatever it takes, you're determined to fill the void He left. Your appetite is insatiable. You eat and eat and eat and eat. It all tastes so good and you find great comfort in the thrill of the taste buds. You can't stop at just one glass of wine. Before you know it you've finished a bottle and are on to the third. Your girlfriends are amazed that you can down six martinis when one used to knock you onto the floor.

Shopping is a magic potion. Every time you make a purchase, the ding of the cash register releases endorphins in your body. You've bought hundreds of new looks for the new you. Nothing is enough. You need that hand-beaded belt, the skirt with the intricate colored stitching, the bright pink sheer blouse that announces you when you step into a room.

You're the ultimate consumer. Advertising executives in boardrooms everywhere drool over the likes of you. You see a commercial with a couple smiling dreamily at each other, and the next thing you know you've switched tampon brands. Your CD and DVD collections have multiplied exponentially. You stand in Pottery Barn and cannot believe how many things you have lived without. You've replaced all the old, ratty frames your pictures were once housed in, you have new area rugs for the living room and dining room, your blinds were getting a bit ragged so you replaced them with nice new wooden slatted sets. Your new couch set looks stunning with the mahogany coffee table you had custom-made.

He walked away from your relationship and left a gaping hole. And you're willing to do whatever it takes to make up for it.

👄 bittergirlspeak

Isn't shopping fun? We love it, and it can be the best therapy. But if you carry on at this rate, not only will you have to get real therapy but you'll be going through bankruptcy too. As we'll talk about later, appearances are important and it's great to have a kick-ass, feel-good outfit to make you feel better. Just ask yourself if you need eighty-nine of those outfits and, if so, where do you plan on wearing them?

Cliché? We Think Not

Before you read any further, no, you are not a cliché. These archetypes have been around for thousands of years. Egyptian hieroglyphics found underneath the mystic palace at Khartoum clearly tell us that Queen Tittenkummen (a lesser-known Egyptian queen) became Angry Girl when she found out her husband was taking three nubile houseslaves with Him into the afterlife, leaving her to guard the entrance to His tomb.

At least today you know right away when you're being dumped. In the little-known diaries of Samuel Pepys's wife, she wrote that her best friend was dumped by a messenger. He had traveled for six months across the seas to deliver the bad news. Ever wonder where the saying "Don't kill the messenger" comes from? Angry Girl.

Choosing Your Bittergirl Team

So, now that you know who you are, you can choose your team appropriately. What do we mean by Choosing Your Team? Well, it's like a sport. Only this time you're not in danger of getting picked last. You're the captain of the team and you get to call the shots. You need a strong offense and a solid defense. You need game plans and

Your Bittergirl Team

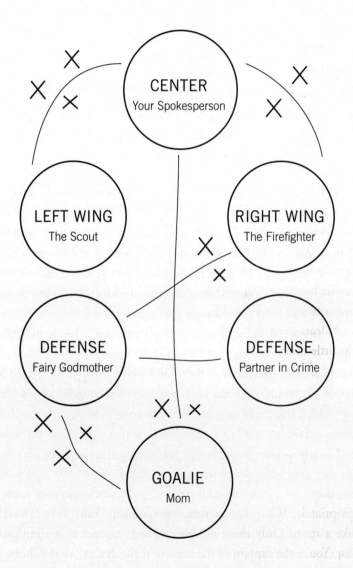

strategies. And what do you hope to win? Your complete self, along with the badge of the bittergirl.

Here's the game plan. Choose among your bestbittergirlfriends to fill the positions. Now, you don't necessarily need six people. You can have two or you can have forty, but you definitely need a team. Sometimes your team members will double up on positions or switch from defense to offense and back again in an evening. Sometimes you'll have one staunch bestbittergirlfriend who fills all the positions single-handedly. However it's constituted, your team stands in front of you and for you through these trying times.

What's a Bestbittergirlfriend?

The bestbittergirlfriend, or BBGF, is someone who doesn't judge or tell you how you should be feeling. She knows that *feelings are facts*. If you're feeling it, it's your truth and it should be respected. Your bestbittergirlfriends listen, they support, and they go to any length to protect and help you through your time of crisis. But not because they have a need to make your drama their own! They're bittergirls at heart and they've been in the trenches themselves.

While it's quite common for your BBGFs to be your immediate friends and family, they can pop up in the most unlikely places. Your dog walker, the crossing guard outside your kid's school, the quiet trainer in HR you used to exchange only smiles with at the coffee station. Listen to your instincts and you'll recognize your BBGFs wherever they are. And sometimes, yes sometimes, those BBGFs can even be male.

Your *Center* is your spokesperson. When you don't have the strength to call and cancel the meeting with your accountant for your joint tax return filing, your Center will make that call or will show up in your place with all your bank statements and pay stubs in order.

She'll call your extended circle of friends so you won't have to yet. She is the public face of your breakup and will keep your life moving forward even though you yourself might be at a standstill. Quite a gal.

The two *Wingers* have very different functions. One forward is your *Right Wing,* your Firefighter. She puts out fires, makes decisions, calls the bank and the telephone company—all the mundane things that you can't possibly hold your head up long enough to deal with. She spots the overdue notices stuffed in your mailbox and sees that the lightbulbs on your front porch are burned out. Then she actually does something about it.

The *Left Wing* is your Lookout, your Scout. She averts potential disasters by making sure He isn't anyplace you want to go. When you first emerge from your cocoon and head to the local liquor store, she'll call to let you know the coast is clear (a particularly valuable function if He hasn't moved out of your neighborhood). And when you finally do go out on the town, she'll go ahead of the team.

This line should give you good offensive coverage.

Now what about your defense? These are your fiercely loyal protectors. Let's start with your two *Defense* positions. On one side there's your Best Fan, aka your Fairy Godmother. She is The Wind Beneath Your Wings. She reminds you of every good thing about you that everyone loves. Every time you see her she greets you with a smile and tells you that you look great. She brings you your favorite pastries from that cute little patisserie you can't get to anymore since you can't leave the house. She holds you and lets you cry like a baby while wiping your tears and nodding. She is the personification of unconditional love: the one who changes your sheets and cleans up around you as you get blown through the maelstrom of Heartbreak Hell. Her presence is akin to a cozy down comforter. She makes you hot chocolate at 3 A.M. and sleeps in your bed so you don't have to be alone.

She's the Fairy Godmother because she magically appears whenever you need her. And you need her.

Mel's live-in guy came home one night with a surprise: He wanted her to move out. As He sprang the news on her, the phone rang. It was her BBGF Ali. Mel said "Hello?" with a quaver in her voice and Ali picked up on it: "Are you all right?" "No." "Is it Jimmy?" "Yes." "Is He breaking up with you?" "Yes!" "Get in a cab and come over— you can stay here and I'll come get your things tomorrow." "Okay— bye." Mel turned to Jimmy and said "That was Ali—she knows everything—I'll be at her place until I find my own apartment." Jimmy never could figure out how Ali knew what was going on almost before He did. Ali is Mel's Fairy Godmother.

Now, your other Defense position is your Partner in Crime, or PIC. Who else will hold your hair back as you puke into a snowbank? Who else will drink those two bottles of cheap wine on a school night just to keep up with you? Your PIC can make you laugh in these dark, dark times. She has a naughty streak, no question, and is probably the one member of your team you can count on to partake in some Bittersweet Revenge. She's also the *only one* who can get away with badmouthing Him: She has immunity because she'll do it with a sense of humor and a quart of tequila in her hand. And she'll never make you feel like she's bad-mouthing you and your choices along with Him.

When Mike walked out on Sarah and the kids, she couldn't figure out how to tell her BBGF Mona on the West Coast. So she sent her a postcard saying, "Well, I've been better: I have a yeast infection, the microwave died, and Mike left me. Love, Sarah." Three days later she came home to a message on her answering machine: "Oh Sarah Sarah Sarah . . . the microwave died?" A few days after that the airline ticket for the Coast arrived in the mail. Mona is Sarah's Partner in Crime.

And finally, we have the *Goalie,* otherwise known as Mom. She's your last and best line of defense against the cold, cruel world. This can actually be your mom, but it doesn't have to be. The Ultimate Truth Sayer, she'll tell everyone else around you exactly what you need and they will listen. She's also the only one who knows when you're ready to hear the unvarnished truth and the only one you'll be able to hear it from. She'll let you have your time, however long it needs to be, and she'll listen patiently. "I could change my job . . . I could move to Halifax . . . I could join the circus . . . I could go away for the holidays . . ." and at just exactly the right moment she'll turn to you and say, "Or you could get over Him." Which will be just what you need to hear.

Okay, baby, you've got your team. Now you have to establish the Rules of Disengagement.

Rules of Disengagement

Rule 1: Milking the Friendship Well

You are going to take advantage of your team. It'll be a one-sided relationship for a while because, frankly, you don't have a whole lot to give right now. You're needy and will pounce on every drop of kindness thrown your way. These are your BBGFs after all, and two years ago you were on Elise's team, and six months from now Patty might need you. Remember, though, that by choosing them to be on your team you've given them permission to tell you the truth. You have to listen. They are your team.

Rule 2: No Dissing Allowed

Your BBGFs cannot mention Him unless you broach the subject first. And once the door is open, only your PIC and your Goalie may speak unkindly of Him. You're already questioning everything you thought you knew about your relationship; hell, your entire life. The last thing you need to question is whether your friends ever liked Him in the first place.

Rule 3: Identify Your Inner and Outer Circles

Miranda your aesthetician might be part of your inner circle but Solange the colorist is so far out on the edge of your outer circle that you don't want her in possession of any potential gossip fodder. If your team knows who your friends are, they can screen your calls and deal with those inner-circle wannabes who are dying to get your breakup on *Jerry Springer*.

Rule 4: Establish Your Lines of Defense

This can change as time goes on, but you must always keep your team abreast of where you are and what you're thinking: What do you want people to know about your breakup? What are you willing to share with the public? This is especially important for your Center. If this were a press release, how would you want it to read? What spin would you put on it? As we'll talk about later, keep in mind that less is more. There's not a lot the world needs to know except that you're no longer together. What the team can focus on is how great you are, even though they just left you lying in three-day-old sweatpants facedown on your bed.

Here are some bittergirl success lines that you might want to try on for size:

> "She's great! You should see her new apartment—she finally got to paint her kitchen that Tuscan Orange she loves."
> "She's great! She and Jenny are walking the Camino in Spain next month."
> "She's great! She was just contacted by someone who's doing a documentary on working mothers who are high achievers."
> "She's great! She's lost three inches off her hips since she took up running."

The focus here should be on moving the subject away from the breakup and on to something positive. Your team can take as many liberties with the truth as is warranted—after all, it's still basically the truth, right?

Rule 5: What's Your Line?
This is the hard one, the one you most need your team's help with. You've come up with the team's press release; now it's time to figure out what *you* want to say. We suggest a three-word line. Short, simple, to the point.

"We broke up."
"He left me."
"It is over."
"Oh, I'm fine."
"Dan? Dan who?"

This line serves a dual purpose. On the one hand, it communicates to others what happened and helps you get used to the idea that you're no longer part of a couple. On the other hand, it's also an affirmation. So although a line like "He fucked [insert name here]" fits the basic parameters, it is more likely to break you down than build you up and definitely leaves the subject wide open to inquiring minds.

When Luke walked out on Sally she got some good advice from a BBGF who told her to keep saying "He left me" until she could say it without crying. It took a few weeks, but eventually she could say it with a smile. Later on someone told Sally they thought it was so great that she was letting the world know in no uncertain terms who left whom. So what had at first made her feel like such a loser later turned into a pretty powerful affirmation. One special BBGF and one kick-ass line.

bitteractivities

1. Write Your Rant   This is a one-shot deal. Write your rant. No holds barred. Write out all the injustices, the feeble excuses, the history that's making you feel like you've failed. Don't worry about grammar or spelling. No one's grading you on this. It's stream of consciousness. Let it all out now, baby. You can stand on a bar stool and shout it out to your team; you can read it out loud to the bathroom mirror and then burn it; you can read it silently to yourself with a bottle of tequila—however you want to approach it, it's your rant.

You could start it off with some simple phrases, like:

I thought He was the one. . . .

I have been dating for sixteen years. . . .

I did not hold on too tight. He let go. . . .

He was the one who persuaded me to fall in love. . . .

I used to go out with a supermodel in Milan, you know. . . .

I wanted to break up with Him two years ago and the bastard convinced me not to. . . .

Everyone says I'm the best thing that ever happened to Him. . . .

2. Practice Your Line   Start small. The mirror. Your teddy bear. Your cat, your dog, your gecko. Then move to the next level. Start on the phone with a telemarketer. Automated billing services at first, then your brother, your aunt, your dad. Soon you can venture into the outside world, baby steps at a time. Practice makes perfect.

3. Game Simulation   Run some plays with your team over a bottle of wine. Set the scene. You're in a bar. Two teammates are with you. He walks in. Plot your strategy. Who does what? Who runs interference? Who's minding the goal? Or, your team is meeting you for lunch. They sit down to find His new flame at the next table. Do they know the drill? Do they have your cell number on speed dial?

4. Practice, Practice, Practice!   Send your team off with home-work. They have to practice *their* lines until they're perfect. Believe the bittergirls: They will be tested.

four

bittergirl breakup
recovery period

LOOK AT YOU. You're doing pretty damn well considering that your life as you knew it has been shattered into a million pieces. You've replayed The Incident, you've named the dumper, you've been present at roll call, and you've even managed to laugh a little bit along the way.

Whether you're conscious of it or not, you're entering the beginning stages of the Bittergirl Breakup Recovery Period, otherwise known as the BBRP. Don't let the word *recovery* fool you though. Right now you're in the earliest stage of the BBRP: the immediate aftermath of The Incident. This is dangerous territory. This is when you'll need your bestbittergirlfriends the most.

Yes, you're determined to maintain your dignity and your pride, to get through this ordeal upright and smiling. After all, you're an honorable member of society, right? You have your bestbittergirlfriends, and you're making a real effort to feel better about things. We know this and we respect you for it, but in the BBRP, never underestimate the moment of weakness that may sucker-punch you when you least expect it. Whether He was an MIA, a Trigger, or a Coward, there's no telling what might happen in that split second when your defenses go down and your vulnerable shell gets a hairline fracture.

This chapter is about preparing yourself for the internationally recognized signals of distress that commonly occur in the BBRP. It's about setting in place an unfailing support system that can help you maintain your dignity even when you don't have your bestbittergirlfriends around to watch out for you. These safeguards may seem completely unreasonable in the light of day when you've just come back from a great workout at the gym or you've flirted with the new bus driver on your route or your son gets a straight-A report card and you know you're succeeding as a single parent. But you will thank the bittergirls when it's 3 A.M. and dark and raining and you're hugging your pillow and crying, or when you finish a bottle of wine while you're in the bath and the water goes cold before you drag yourself out, or when you're on your way home from a party and just happen to find yourself wandering barefoot in His new neighborhood.

Believe the bittergirls: During the early stages of the BBRP, *anything* can happen.

Who knew that a song by Crowded House (which incidentally Cara and Liam *never* listened to in their entire five-year relationship) would compel Cara to bail out of a cab into a snowbank where she sat a sobbing mess trying desperately to punch in Liam's parents' phone number? At the time it seemed perfectly normal to her that she should phone them at midnight on a Tuesday and find out if they knew what Liam was thinking or whether He'd ever come back to her. Luckily for Cara, Susie was with her. Susie recognized the distress signals, confiscated her cell phone, hailed another cab, and made sure Cara got home and to bed without drinking and dialing.

The signals of distress are many, too many to list in full, so we've culled the tomes at The Bittergirl Institute for Advanced Research on Dumping and come up with the top ten.

top ten internationally recognized signals of distress

1. A desperate need for chocolate
2. The ability to drink copious amounts of Scotch without ever getting drunk
3. Sudden urges to destroy His personal property, followed by desperate attempts to piece it back together
4. Checking voicemail every two minutes to see if He's called
5. The overwhelming urge to sit in His bushes at midnight to see if He comes home alone
6. Calling His office after hours just to hear His voice on His voicemail
7. Hiring a plane to write "PLEASE come back to me" in the sky
8. Taking out ad time on your local radio station to send Him messages
9. Pulling the fire alarm at His apartment building just so you can see Him
10. The inability to finish a sentence without saying His name

Now that you're aware of the top ten Internationally Recognized Signals of Distress, don't think you can easily avoid them. If you must enact one or more of the IRSOD, try to do it in private or only in front of your bestbittergirlfriends. This is what we like to call Keeping Up Appearances.

Keeping Up Appearances

KUA is one of the most crucial aspects of the BBRP. Yes, you may have had some blips already—that little public sobbing incident in the contraceptive aisle of the drugstore, the time you went to McDonald's by yourself with greasy hair and no bra, or the time you freaked out and screamed at the strange woman standing on His doorstep at 4 A.M. until you realized it was the paper delivery girl. All these things are acceptable *once*, but the idea is to try to keep the oh-so-inevitable-very-emotional outbursts to the confines of safe company. KUA is what keeps your public life going while your private life has crumbled like a stale potato latke.

Now, you might think you'll never voluntarily leave the house again. But you will, and that's why you need the SOS Safety Measures. These measures may save you the embarrassment of showing up at the front door of His recently acquired house at 2 A.M. holding a new line of allergy medication because you know His allergies bug Him at this time of year. Or baking His favorite cookies and barging into a deal-breaking meeting in the boardroom of His office. Or waking up hungover on a Thursday morning with the phone receiver cradled in your neck and that icky feeling that you phoned Him and said some things you are most definitely going to regret.

"Really," you're probably saying, "I think I've got it under control. I know I feel worse when I talk to Him and so I just shouldn't." But seriously, as the bittergirls know from painful experience, you can never anticipate when hormones, alcohol, chocolate, memories, loneliness, or bloodlust will take over and you'll find yourself hurtling toward near disaster. It may feel as though your iron will is never going to bend under the pressure, but even iron eventually bends, melts, and forms a puddle when sufficiently heated. And the less time you find yourself in puddle formation, the better.

The reality is that in the immediate aftermath of the breakup you will miss Him. You'll be reminded of Him every day by even the most ridiculous morsels of life that had absolutely nothing to do with Him. You'll feel like your world has ended, that you'll never get over this or Him for that matter, that life is so utterly unfair. You'll promise to never ever let yourself get hurt again. In fact, you may just never love again.

All these feelings and the million others that go along with the end of a relationship will shift and fluctuate depending on the moon, the news, or whether you have that burnt chocolate marshmallow ice cream in your freezer. According to The Bittergirl Institute for Advanced Research on Dumping, the emotional stress a woman experiences after the loss of a relationship is second only to the pain of losing a loved one. Note: You did just lose a loved one. He just isn't dead. Now it may be a bitter pill to swallow, but we bittergirls are here to remind you of the good news in this horrible time: You still have a pulse. Granted, it may feel a bit faint, but with the aid of the SOS Safety Measures and the Contract that follows, it will slowly return to its vibrant, throbbing fullness (a vibrator may help matters too).

This is the chapter you MUST COME BACK TO when everything is falling apart. And, honey, at some point it will fall apart. Put these provisions in place, though, and you'll be helping yourself before you even know you need it.

SOS Safety Measures

These must-dos and must-haves will help see you through the early stages of the Bittergirl Breakup Recovery Period. This preventative system is here to set you up to withstand any long-term trip to Hermitland.

Phone Zone

While a fabulously convenient tool for communication, the phone can also be an instrument of devastation during the BBRP. Take heed of this very important bittergirl advice.

Reset Your Speed Dial   Take Him off it *completely*—both on your home phone AND your cell phone. You are going to need your BBGFs and the nearest pizza delivery store programmed in; then your mother, your gay neighbor, and a cab company that can take you to one of your BBGFs' houses.

It may be easy for some bittergirls-in-training to deprogram His phone number, but you may find yourself with no backbone, no willpower, no desire to even want to stop yourself from phoning. If you're in the latter category, call in the troops. Either station yourself at one of your bestbittergirlfriends' places (if you're not living there already while you look for your new fabulous apartment) or ask one of them to station themselves at yours. Surrender your cell phone. After dark, make her unplug and confiscate all the phones in the house except for the room she's in. This may sound drastic, but studies done by The Bittergirl Institute for Advanced Research on Dumping show that one is five times more likely to give in to emotional and irrational behavior after dark. That's when loneliness usually hits.

You may curse your bestbittergirlfriend now, but, as you'll learn from abiding by the Contract at the end of this chapter, having NO direct contact with Him really is in your best interest. Note: You may wish to introduce heavy bouts of swearing at this time. This is encouraged where appropriate, and due to its cathartic nature is often fully recommended.

Resist the desire to program a horoscope or psychic line into your speed dial. As one of our bittergirls found out, it's not so nice to get a two-hundred-dollar phone bill because you wanted to see if there were any new planetary developments.

Add Space to Your Voicemail Box   This will allow you to let the phone go unanswered for long periods of time without your callers hearing "The mailbox you are trying to reach is full." Your friends might understand, but you want to Keep Up Appearances. You may be sitting at home watching *I Love Lucy* reruns, but other people don't have to know that. All a full mailbox says to them is "My life is falling apart." It may very well be, but, again, other people don't have to know. Remember, KUA.

Get Caller ID   This may cost a little more each month, but it's essential for your sanity. After all, you may not want to talk to your mom for the fortieth time today, but you definitely don't want to miss the pizza delivery guy when he's calling from your doorstep with your steaming hot comfort food.

   DO NOT TRY TO RERECORD YOUR ANSWERING MACHINE MESSAGE AT THIS TIME. Simply choose the generic electronic greeting—believe us, that's what they're there for. No one needs to hear you sobbing as you try to explain that He isn't living in your apartment anymore or screaming to the heavens that His calls can be forwarded at the cost of one Office Bitch's life.

The Emergency Kit

There are certain essential comforts that a bittergirl turns to in times of heartbreak. The Emergency Kit contains a few items we deem necessities during the BBRP.

Food   Bittergirls have been known to use food as an emotional substitute—to forget, to ease the pain, to numb the mind, to avoid falling into a lonely abyss. Now if this persists for any length of time, we'll need to talk. Meanwhile, it is entirely fine to cuddle up to a bag of Doritos or a pint of ice cream every once in a while if it's going to make you feel better.

A true bittergirl keeps a well-stocked kitchen for these occasions.

bittergirl top tasters

Fridge: A can of ready-made chocolate icing, a tub of good olives, six bottles of Chardonnay

Freezer: Two quarts of vodka, a pint of vanilla fudge caramel ice cream, prepackaged frozen macaroni and cheese

Cupboard: A large bag of Cool Ranch Doritos, backup bottle of Scotch

Sunglasses   Imperative to hide those puffy, swollen eyes, the sadness in your pupils, the swelling tears that might take you unawares.

Clothes   The basic essentials include a well-loved flannel bathrobe, comfy pajamas, and the puffiest slippers around. These popular BBRP garments have proven their mettle. If you do go out of the house, be sure you wear a baseball cap to cover the unbrushed, unwashed hair. Put on your favorite jeans and a top that can pass as clean, and don't forget underwear and a bra. Going commando may be sexy, but not under these circumstances.

This is where KUA comes in. You're not thinking clearly during this time, so plan ahead and establish one steadfast outfit you can throw on if you need to leave the house. If you can't decide on an outfit, make your bestbittergirlfriend lay one out for you in a highly visible place. Leeza, a charter bittergirl, didn't plan ahead and ended up walking to the post office to mail a letter in her bathrobe and slippers. Luckily it was 3 A.M., the post office was closed, and no one saw her, but you get the picture. Eventually you'll have to expand your wardrobe, but that's for another chapter and another day.

Books and Magazines   Pamper yourself. Order those trashy novels and magazines you've so often gazed at but were too embarrassed to be seen reading. This is no time for shame. This is a time for guilty pleasures, anything to help you get through. Take Catherine, who went online and bought every self-help book on the market. She diligently completed every self-affirming, self-discovery, self-confidence-building exercise and went on to write her own self-help book. Pick up one of the novels on your bookshelf you've been meaning to read for years. And if the great classics are too deep to wade through, there's no end of funny, heartwarming, soul-filling, trashy girly books you can dive into and get lost in. Besides, reading is a great way to trick yourself into forgetting about how many hours have passed since The Incident. Before you know it, you'll have finished a shelf of Harlequin romances and not only will Fabio have replaced Him in your daydreams, three months may just have passed.

Movies   Always have your local video-store card ready for your best-bittergirlfriend to use, and put out a recall of all the cheesy movies you've lent to people in the past. It's time to establish a fully stocked movie library. Right now it's perfectly okay to watch *Some Kind of Wonderful, Pretty in Pink, St. Elmo's Fire,* or *Sleepless in Seattle* over and over and over again. *It's a Wonderful Life* works even when it's the middle of summer. Movies are a great escape and an effective way of getting those salty teardrops out of your system. Who cares if you've watched *Gone with the Wind* 422 times? It's your life.

Television   GET CABLE!

movies and tv to distract you or help get your anger out

film noir
anything with Jackie Chan
anything with Harrison Ford
James Bond movies
Sex and the City (an entire season)
The Sopranos
Thelma and Louise
Kill Bill Vol. 1 and Vol. 2
Reservoir Dogs
XXX
Rocky
Mission: Impossible
pretty much anything where stuff gets blown up
Terminator and *Terminator 2*
Norma Rae
Silkwood
The China Syndrome
The Manchurian Candidate (1962)

movies to cry to

The Way We Were
Truly Madly Deeply
Some Kind of Wonderful
Endless Love
Casablanca
The English Patient
Roman Holiday

Love Story
The Power of One
The Killing Fields
Finding Nemo
Whale Rider
The French Lieutenant's Woman

movies and tv to make you feel good

It's a Wonderful Life
The Philadelphia Story
Holiday
Legally Blonde
Airplane
Top Secret
the *Pink Panther* movies
The Party
Waiting for Guffman (or anything by Christopher Guest)
Saturday Night Live (the early seasons)
Laverne and Shirley
The Mary Tyler Moore Show
The Dick Van Dyke Show
The Jeffersons (sing that theme song!)
Happy Days

movies that twist the knife

Love, Actually
An Affair to Remember

Sleepless in Seattle
Breakfast at Tiffany's
Sliding Doors
Emma
Pride and Prejudice
Good Will Hunting
An Officer and a Gentleman
Pretty Woman
Shrek and *Shrek 2*
Beauty and the Beast
The Princess Bride
Four Weddings and a Funeral

Music   Anything goes. From John Denver to Blondie to Zeppelin. Whatever you need to listen to, AS LONG AS IT WASN'T A "SPECIAL" SONG FOR THE TWO OF YOU. We advise clearing out the CDs of all those indie bands you went to see at the beginning of your relationship, along with the one that reminds you of the first time you made love, the one you listened to as you danced in front of the Christmas tree, or the one He made for you to listen to as you ran your first marathon. Throw them in a cardboard box, cart them down to the local CD shop, and TRADE THEM IN! You're creating a new life for yourself. You want music that fills your soul or doesn't remind you of Him, or that gets you angry enough that you don't want to call Him. Begin your new, very own collection of YOUR MUSIC. Explore the African drumming or world music section or fall back into your Pat Benatar days.

music to make you feel good

"Lady Marmalade"

The Barenaked Ladies

Duran Duran

Wham!

Motown

ABBA

Ella Fitzgerald

anything by Louis Prima

'80s girl groups

'60s girl groups

Grease soundtrack

music to wallow in

Blue (the whole album) by Joni Mitchell

Sarah McLachlan ("I Will Remember You"—over and over)

"The Way We Were" by Barbra Streisand

"Crazy for You" by Madonna

anything by Nina Simone

Dusty Springfield (pretty much anything)

anything by Lionel Ritchie or Air Supply

"I Wanna Know What Love Is" by Foreigner

"Nobody Knows Me Like My Baby" by Lyle Lovett

Kenny Rogers or John Denver

"Sorry Seems to Be the Hardest Word" by Elton John

"Wonderful Tonight" by Eric Clapton

"One Less Bell to Answer" by Burt Bacharach

Roxy Music

music to kick ass to

"I Will Survive" (it's the anthem, baby) by Gloria Gaynor

Jagged Little Pill (the whole CD) by Alanis Morissette

"Keep Me Hangin' On" by Kim Wilde

"Shattered Glass" (Kim again)

"Don't Let Me Get Me" by Pink

The Clash

"Walking on Broken Glass" by Annie Lennox

The Eurythmics

Ani DiFranco

Guns N' Roses

Bon Jovi

The Sex Pistols

Blondie

Journal   We only write when things are bad. There's a reason why we wrote bad poetry in high school and why our teenage journals were filled with heartache and heartbreak and angst and drama. We need to get it out and sometimes paper is the only way. There are so many reasons why writing down what you're feeling can help, but the main one is to help maintain your dignity. In your journal you can breathe fire, wreak revenge, call Him every name under the sun, and purge everything you're thinking. Whether the tears are falling faster than the ink is flowing or you're so angry that you're afraid the nib is going to break, nothing judges you less than your very own journal.

And if you're writing about what you're going through, chances are you might go back and read some of it and gain a bit of perspective on the situation. Or, if you're like Adrienne, you can just write and write and write until there's nothing left for you to say and then burn the pages so no one can ever hold you to those words. Whatever your fancy, let it all out.

Vibrator (Or the Next Best Thing)   Get a vibrator—if you don't have one, go out right now and buy one. Nowhere in your small town to get one? What do you think the Internet is for? Mail order!

If buying a vibrator is not a step you're ready to take, at least get yourself a very powerful removable shower nozzle with a number of different water massage settings. Many a bittergirl has been known to spend hours crying in the shower—not from heartbreak but from happiness at discovering a multiorgasmic showerhead. We won't go into gory details, but suffice it to say that your local hardware store is bound to have a wide array of nozzles of happiness.

Punching Bag   Blow up a picture of Him and paste it on the bag. Self-explanatory.

Tissues   Buy the store out. And be sure to get the ones with moisturizer involved. No one needs to deal with The Incident AND dry, cracking under-the-nose skin.

The Contract

The next step is Signing the Contract, and it's a tough step to take because it implies accountability. Every bittergirl who reads this book and truly wants to move on signs a contract. The key words here are "wants to move on." As you may have witnessed while stranded in heartbreak hell, there are some people who just want to stay there. They velcro themselves to anyone else who's been dumped and beg them to dwell in this fiery oblivion—misery loves company, right?

No. A true self-respecting bittergirl realizes that while it's important to mourn the relationship, it's just as important to recognize that at some point you need to move on. By signing this Contract, you're making a deal with yourself that will help you go forward. It will remind you in moments of weakness that you have your best interests in mind and it will make you responsible for your actions. If you break the Contract, you're breaking a deal with yourself. And then who can you blame?

So, read it carefully and bite the bullet. Think of how good, no, *heavenly*, it will be to feel yourself starting to get over this.

You must abide by the rules of this contract at ALL TIMES, regardless of how drunk, how tired, how emotional, how frustrated, how angry, how horny, how desperate you are. A month may seem like forever, but by the time it passes and you've held true to this Contract, we guarantee you'll be well on your way to being a true bittergirl.

The Bittergirl Institute for Advanced Research on Dumping has discerned a directly inverse relationship between the time it takes to heal a broken heart and the amount of contact with its perpetrator. In bittergirlspeak: If you don't talk to Him, you'll get over Him faster.

Now that you've signed the Contract and had a good friend stand witness, hang it in a prominent place in your abode. The bittergirls even suggest making numerous copies and pasting them beside every phone in the house. Anytime you feel a shift in your foundation—you start thinking about all the important things that you really, really need to tell Him, the crack in the pavement widening and threatening to swallow you up, your mask of dignity slowly slipping—remember KUA. IMMEDIATELY contact your closest friend, reread your Contract, and head for the emergency kit. *You are not well right now—you need help.* There's no shame in asking for it.

BITTERGIRL CONTRACT

I, _____, hereby agree to abide by the following rules for one
month from today, this _____ of _____, _____.

1. I must not, under any circumstances, call Him.
2. I repeat, I must not, under any circumstances, call Him.
3. I must not, under any circumstances, get drunk and call Him.
4. I must not, under any circumstances, call His family.
5. I must not, under any circumstances, call His friends.
6. I must not, under any circumstances, return His calls.
7. I must not, under any circumstances, save His message if He does
   call.
8. I must not, under any circumstances, e-mail Him.
9. I must not, under any circumstances, drive by His new place.
10. I must not, under any circumstances, go to His work.
11. I must not, under any circumstances, go to His gym.
12. I must not, under any circumstances, frequent His favorite bar.
13. I must not, under any circumstances, read any of His old letters.
14. I must not, under any circumstances, bring out "our" old photos.
15. I must not, under any circumstances, listen to "our" music.
16. I must not, under any circumstances, CALL HIM!

Signed: _____

Witness: _____

Skip the following if you don't have kids.

Subcontract: If you must have contact with him because of daycare
arrangements, kids' schedules, or the like, add the following disclaimer

17. I will call him only if it directly relates to an emergency regarding our
    child/children.

Signed: _____

Witness: _____

or refer to the Bittermoms chapter to sign your subcontract.

That's why you've taken all the SOS Safety Measures. You're going to come through this and you're going to be better than fine. You've got the bittergirls with you.

And just in case the prospect of sheer humiliation isn't enough for you, we would like to share a couple of stories.

Take Alice. She tried to erase John's number from her speed dial but it was just too hard. Besides, she was convinced she wouldn't weaken and phone Him. She was dealing with it all so well. She was just keeping His number there until she felt "ready" to erase it. Well, after attending a high school buddy's wedding (solo) one Saturday night, Alice was overwhelmed with loneliness, with memories of dancing with John at His brother's wedding and of planning what their first song would be on their own wedding day. Her will weakened and crumbled. She dialed. John answered groggily, and just as Alice was about to spill her heart out, she heard a woman's voice: "Who is it, honey?"

Or Wendy, who was sitting in the waiting room at her gynecologist's office and overheard two women talking. One of them was recounting the tale of a friend's coworker whose ex-girlfriend had phoned and hung up 162 times in one hour. The situation had become so ridiculous that He had His number changed and unlisted. Wendy felt so good because *finally* someone else was calling an ex just as much if not more than she was calling Owen. Then she realized that the person they were talking about *was* Owen. Ouch.

As all bittergirls know, hindsight is said to be 20/20. It's unlikely that when you were in the throes of your passionate love affair you wanted to see that The Louse was The Louse, or you would have had your house decontaminated before He set foot in it. Likewise, you would have already had a career change planned for The Mountie when He threw His midlife crisis at you. But the vision this chapter hopes to encourage is foresight. We've learned from our mistakes and we want to prevent our fledgling bittergirl from any unnecessary set-backs. You've been kicked in the teeth already. Don't provide the boots to get kicked again. Don't pull a Wendy on us.

So stay in as much as you want, screen those calls, watch those movies, read the trashy magazines, eat the cupboards bare, drain the liquor cabinet, lean on the team—whatever it takes to get you through right now. But DO NOT MAKE CONTACT WITH HIM. We promise that if you use the SOS Safety Measures and adhere to the Contract during this initial stage of the BBRP, you may feel like one hell of a hermit but might just have spared yourself some mighty humiliations. And you'll be one step closer to Renavigating Your Life.

 bitteractivities

1. Write Your Own Contract   Get your bestbittergirlfriends to help you with this one, and outline major pitfalls you need to avoid.

2. Create Your Own Emergency Kit   Fill it with your favorite comfort foods, songs, movies, books, etc.

five

renavigating your life

So at this point in your BBRP you've been dealing with the bare necessities of living. Sure you're only getting by on one or two of the basic food groups, you likely haven't seen sunlight for days, and you probably feel light-headed from a lack of fresh air and too much Chardonnay. You may be horizontal, but you are breathing. Your heart may still be numb, but there is some functioning brain activity. You've made it through the initial stages of the BBRP and signed the Contract. You've acknowledged that you're going to have to find a way to get over this. You've bought the finest Belgian chocolate and have another chilled bottle of Chardonnay in front of you and several more in the fridge. You have all of this month's glossies, an embarrassingly sexy bodice ripper, and a DVD of the latest chick flick. Your cell phone is under lock and key and you haven't played "your" song once all day.

Oh lamb, who are you kidding? You can't keep on like this. Can you honestly differentiate between yesterday and today? Quick! Name three things going on in the world that have nothing to do with your breakup. Come on, this is not a life. And for your sake and sanity, this is not a reality you can stay in. It's time to wash that man right out of your hair by Renavigating Your Life.

Housebound

No matter how He dumped you, no matter the reason and no matter how you've been coping with it, at some point you're going to have to leave the house. We don't mean leaving to go and pick up more booze and frozen pizza or the daily trek to the office and straight home to the duvet, we mean rejoining the human race. If we hadn't gone through it ourselves we wouldn't suggest it. But we know the colossal importance of rebuilding your life when you can no longer remember what the point of your life was.

When you're feeling raw and rejected it's hard to believe that to the rest of the universe you're essentially the same you that you were before you met Him and the you that you'll be when you're over Him. The difficult part is remembering who that you is, and how to get her back. Don't fret. The bittergirls are here to help.

When so much of your day-to-day life has been as part of a couple, the idea of getting back out there may seem easier said than done. You and He were working toward a future, whether you were following a five-year plan, preparing for retirement, or deciding if it was time to meet the parents. Doesn't matter. The fact is, that future has been altered and now it's looming right in front of you.

How to rejoin the human race when your heart is broken? Easy. Open the front door. Go for a walk. Buy milk at the shop that's three blocks away from your place instead of the one that's closest. If you aren't up for crazy nights out with your pals, bring a book to a local café. Go window-shopping. Go to a movie, a museum, a local library. Look up an old friend. Try to remember something you used to enjoy that didn't involve Him. Go and do it.

Now hopefully you weren't one of those women (and don't we all know at least one) who dropped her entire life the moment she got her man. Hopefully you're still in touch with the friends you had pre-Him and still have at least an interest or two outside the daily domesticity of the life you shared. If not, let this be a lesson for next time. No matter how in love or lust you are, do not give your entire self away no matter how wonderful He is.

What about signing up for a class or developing a new hobby? Now, before you pooh-pooh that idea, think of the advantages. You'll meet a group of entirely new people who've never known you as "the other half." This is a chance to meet others as an interesting, independent woman. You'll open up your social circle to people with a similar interest. You'll amaze your bestbittergirlfriends with your Japanese cooking skills at your first bittergirls' night in and maybe replace some of those ceramics you destroyed in the early days of your BBRP. Developing an interest in something besides your breakup prevents you from becoming Beyond Bitter and brings you one step closer to reclaiming your Kernel. It will eat up the hours before you can go to bed and the weekends that lie before you. Isn't that incentive enough?

When Ella got dumped she didn't know what to do with herself. Walking past an arts supply store on one of her solitary evening strolls she saw a sign in the window advertising a painting class for beginners. Now Ella hadn't lifted a paintbrush since high school art, but she registered anyway. In the months that followed, the class became more than just something to take up time. She developed a talent she never knew she possessed and gave a whole new meaning to Painting Him Out of Your Life.

When Antonia got dumped she nursed her wounds for months on end. After bemoaning the state of her love life, her boredom with her job, and her desire to travel, she figured the next best thing to meeting the perfect guy, getting the dream job, and having an adventure would be to sign up for a kickboxing class at the local YMCA. Months later, toned, confident, and with a killer kick, she laughed and said the breakup was the best thing that ever happened to her health and self-esteem. When a job opened up at her company's offices in Martinique, Antonia leapt at the opportunity and the change of scenery. Two out of three ain't bad, she figured.

I'm Ready for My Close-up

We've already stressed the importance of Keeping Up Appearances. Hopefully you're over the spontaneous sobbing in public, but now more than ever you need to make that extra effort with your physical appearance. But beware: Looking good is not about getting Him back. It's about remembering who you were before you met Him. By Renavigating Your Life you're putting on a brave face and showing the world that He didn't break you. So first step, remove the robe or the yoga pants you've been wearing for the last week and a half. Grab a member of your team and go shopping (yes, even if you don't feel like it). Do not come home without a pair of knee-high fuck-me boots or a pair of sexy kitten heels. Can't afford to? Sweetie, right now you can't afford not to.

It's all about attitude, and The Bittergirl Institute for Advanced Research on Dumping indicates that women most definitely walk with attitude in the above-mentioned footwear. And nine out of ten landlords polled admit to giving the woman in the fuck-me boots a better deal on rent than her male counterpart. If possible, get your hair done. Buy some new makeup and toiletries. We know this isn't going to cure your broken heart but we'll be damned if you're going to look like hell just because you're feeling that way.

The bittergirls remember bumping into Trigger's friend at a party.

He confided in Trigger's ex that all His buddies couldn't believe how amazing she looked, and what had he been thinking? Total cost of looking fabulous? Attitude. Or take a lesson from Meg's book. When her fiancé left her at the altar (He was playing a spoon and fell in love with a plate in a touring musical that shall remain nameless to protect the parties involved) she returned her wedding dress and spent the refund on two drop-dead gorgeous sundresses. Her veil went into storage and she cut the long hair He'd loved into a gamine look that announced her new identity. If she was crying on the inside no one outside her team saw it.

It doesn't matter that right now you don't care if another man ever sees you barefoot; it matters that you know you have a nice pedicure. KUA is about grabbing self-love wherever you can get it—even if that means a little loofah and some polish in front of the shopping channel. If one out of ten nice things you do for yourself works, consider yourself successful.

Your Adoring Public

We've been that heaving wreck on the floor. We've been that woman weeping as she mouths the words along to late-night infomercials. And we recognize that sometimes the idea of getting back into the land of the living seems about as painless as running a marathon. Hell, just getting out of bed in the morning feels like running a marathon both hungover and needing to pee. Scaling Mount Kilimanjaro in heels is more appealing than the thought of stepping out the front door and facing your life. The cameras, the flashes, the vulturelike questions of the paparazzi desperate to know why He called it off—excuse us, but we have a sneaking suspicion that, although it may feel that way, there are no cameras outside your door.

One of us had to start rehearsals for our play *bittergirl* the morning after getting dumped. Did we know the show would turn into a smash hit and that we'd perform it in places like New York and London? Did we ever anticipate using our experiences to write this book? No, we simply leaned on each other, put one foot in front of the other, and remained open to whatever the day brought. And baby, it brought more than that sorry son of a bitch ever could have. So not only are you going to begin reclaiming your life, you're going to do it with style, flair, and dignity. Starting now.

So it's Saturday night, Sunday morning, or Tuesday afternoon. You could go to that party, that picnic, that jog in the park. But you don't. What's the point? Leaving the house means walking the streets with a neon sign over your head that screams "I just got dumped." It's easier and safer to just stay under the covers than risk the public humiliation, right? Imagine the jokes Uncle Joe will make or the pitying stares from little Henrick's Scout leader.

In the months following her breakup Lucie hid in her apartment at night, missing Him and examining where it all went wrong. She went through her days as though she had a flashing light above her screaming "I'M NOT GOOD/SEXY/SMART/PRETTY ENOUGH." It took her by surprise when she realized that she was actually ashamed at having been dumped. She imagined what people were saying about the demise of the "perfect couple." Dear Lucie, remember that old saying "Pride goeth before a fall"?

Nope, there's nothing like having to go out there and admit yet another failed relationship.

And there's nothing we bittergirls hate more than the term *failed relationship*. The relationship didn't "fail," honey, it ended. Failing is not trying. Failing is hiding away while your life goes on without you. Failing is letting this breakup identify you. You're so much more than "she who just got dumped." That may be hard to remember at 3 A.M. sitting on the edge of the bathtub and sobbing into His sweater, but believe the bittergirls: The strangers you pass on the street don't know He dumped you unless you tell them. You didn't get dumped by everyone else in your life, so to them you're still you. Right now it may seem like your world is full of prying eyes—your boss, your upstairs neighbor, your mother's hairdresser—desperate for a soundbite in the tawdry saga that was once your relationship.

But let us remind you that you're under no obligation to provide the dirty details. Now that you're finally resurfacing from the Hermitland you visited in the initial stages of the BBRP, you probably need to review your line from Chapter 3. You're going to run into people. They're going to bellow at you across the grocery store: "Oh-my-god-I-haven't-seen-you-since-Chris-left-what-on-earth-happened?!" Let us reiterate. A line as simple as "It didn't work out" is all people ever need to get the point that it's really none of their business. Remember, you're reentering your life with self-respect, not as some woman scorned. You got dumped. That's the only thing different about you. You're still a sister, a daughter, a mother, an accountant, a trapeze artist, a bad speller, a great cook, a backgammon champion. He's not your only topic of conversation and He's not what defines you. Your breakup will be news for about five minutes until your brother gets arrested for possession, Jenny from HR announces her pregnancy by the stockboy, or your dad's hip starts acting up again. People are too busy with their own lives to spend more than a fleeting moment worrying about yours.

That said, while your sister loves you and your mother worries you aren't eating, they simply can't know exactly what you're feeling as you go through your BBRP and start to Renavigate Your Life. You're mourning your loss and trying to get over the memories you created together, and they can't share that no matter how they try. Those around you are probably well intentioned and only want you to be okay, so you're going to have to cut them some slack. On those days when you can't get out of bed, your bestbittergirlfriend may think a little tough love or "Rise and Shine" is all you need. It's agonizing but you have to tolerate it. If you're going to have a meltdown at her Thanksgiving dinner, cry on her shoulder, and cancel plans at the last minute, your team gets to be a little bossy with you once in a while.

Do You Know the Way to San Jose?

Leaving the confines of your house in the aftermath of a breakup involves navigating a veritable minefield of emotional kryptonite. You won't be able to control everything, but you can take measures to manage a lot of it.

Is He still the first thing you think about every morning? Then you need to think about Renavigating Your Day. It won't make you forget the gaping hole where your heart used to be, but getting off the subway one stop sooner on your way to work may just change the scenery and serve as a reminder that life is indeed happening all around you.

If you normally had dinner together every night and can't face the emptiness of an evening alone, change the routine. Why not head to the gym after work? Join a hot yoga class? Take up rock climbing? Not into working out? Use this time to run errands or catch up on the work you missed earlier in your BBRP. Become a big sister, volunteer at a literacy program or a drop-in center. Just do something that gets you out of the routine you shared. It can also help put your relationship problems into perspective.

When one bittergirl found the dinner hour too painful to go home to, she arranged to pick her granddaughter up from daycare each day and spent a blissful few hours playing with her. Her family was grateful for the extra help, and for those few hours she could almost forget that her husband of thirty years had walked out. Another bittergirl remembers, "I couldn't help wondering if He was across town drinking our juice and reading our newspaper in the mornings. Was He reading the exact words I was at that moment? What did He think of the editorial?" In bittergirl fashion she eventually started drinking cranberry instead of orange juice and switched newspapers. Small steps to be sure, but she no longer spends her mornings obsessing over pulp and prepositions.

When your BBRP is ticking away oh-so-slowly, the thought of empty evenings, weekends, or holidays can be overwhelming. Take matters into your own hands and decide how you want to spend that time. Maybe last week you felt like some alone time, and maybe next week you'll want to be surrounded by other people. See how you're feeling, then get on the phone and make some plans. Saturday night may be less daunting if you know that on Tuesday you're meeting a friend for dinner at that new Thai place.

What a Tangled Web We Weave

If you were married or cohabiting, there are going to be leases, mortgages, utilities, and other financial entanglements that will need attending to. Do not put this off. This is yet another of those situations when your Spokesperson or your Firefighter get to prove why they're the best team players around. Write a list of what needs dealing with. Ask one of them to find out how the necessary changes need to be made. The institution won't release any confidential information, but they will provide the basic procedures and you won't have to spend the morning on the phone explaining for the umpteenth time between sobs that "He lef, He lef, He left me. . . ." Most industries (with the exception of the wedding trade and the airlines) are sympathetic to the dissolution of a relationship. No, they'll still want your mortgage payment on time, but they may help you change the payment routine.

Yielding the Harvest

There's a reason Canada is consistently ranked one of the best places to live in the world, and it ain't Medicare. It's called Grocery Gateway, and honey, it may just save your life. Many people don't recognize the value of this national treasure until they're having to avoid all those damned smug couples gazing into each other's eyes as they stroll through the market, brie and baguettes in hand. If you don't live in a city where you can order your groceries online and have them delivered dirt cheap, there are other options that will allow you to avoid coming face to face with THE LIFE THAT USED TO BE YOURS. Do not under any circumstances go grocery shopping on a weekend or immediately after work. This is emotional torture. It is the persecution of the heartbroken gal. The last thing you need at this point in your recovery are happy families openly taunting you with their domestic bliss as you toss another single-serving "Memories of Monaco" into your lonely little basket for one.

How much do you want to bet that the first twenty-four-hour grocery store was opened by a bittergirl sick of the smug smiles of the domesticated? Shop on Monday mornings. Don't cruise your produce aisles until you're ready to really start cruising again.

Parting Is Such Sweet Sorrow

It's a miserable fact that just because some louse dumped you, you're forced to say goodbye to a number of people who've become vital to your happiness. Nobody treats your cashmere quite like Mr. Lee from the dry cleaners and not a soul can tame your brows like Sonia and her House of Beauty, but if any of these lifelines are close to His house, His office, His parents' place, or the restaurant where He proposed, or even have the same color walls as the paint chips you looked at that weekend at the hardware store, you're inviting the emotional floodgates to open in the worst way imaginable. If there's even the slightest chance that you may bump into Him—or that Sonia's new aesthetician Freddie wears the same cologne as He does or that Mr. Lee will ask if He was happy with how he treated His French cuffs— thank them for the memories and walk away. You do not want a Bittergirl Breakdown at this point in your recovery. Yes, it's going to be near impossible to find a hairdresser who'll cut your bangs just right, but it's going to be a lot easier than growing out the hatchet job you'll commit on your poor locks after a brick from memory lane wallops you on the side of the head.

If at all possible, stay away from His side of the tracks until you're emotionally healthy and well and truly over Him. If you're in one of those exceptionally horrendous situations where you have to see Him or one of His friends, family, or business colleagues, go straight to Chapter 12: "Bittergirl Breakdown," memorize it, then tear the chapter out and carry it in your purse at all times. If you must see Him due to custody arrangements, it may help to have one of your BBGFs (preferably your Fairy Godmother or your Mom) on standby in the kitchen so that after you close the door smiling and waving to your children, you can collapse into her arms. If you're like Molly and have to walk past His office every day on your way to the boardroom, you may also want to keep emergency measures in your purse. These include waterproof mascara, a journal, a miniature of Bailey's, and a large pair of dark Jackie-O sunglasses.

In your effort to Renavigate Your Life, you may discover that some conveniences are so necessary to your day that you simply cannot let Him have them. This is what is known as a . . .

Turf War

Got a favorite coffee shop that happens to be in His neighborhood? Order yourself six extra-large lattes and sit in the window seat every day for a week straight. Bring a good book so that you aren't tempted to peek out and look for Him. If He doesn't see you there, hopefully one of His buddies will and declare the joint off limits. Don't want to look that aimless? Stop in on your way to work and tell your sordid story to your favorite bittergirl barista. The next time He's in, He'll get the cold shoulder with His cold Americana.

To gain squatting rights at your favorite watering hole, you'll need the help of your Scout and the rest of your BBGF team. You should not be seeing Him in your weakened state, particularly if there's alcohol involved. So send rotating groups of pals to the pub in your place. (It may give them incentive if you offer to pay for the first few rounds.) When He spots them and sheepishly asks how you're doing, instruct them carefully to employ their game plan from Chapter 3 and coolly say things like "She's fine. We invited her out, but she already had plans." Coach them until they can say it breezily in three different languages. Backward if necessary. Think Gestapo tactics here. Place your team anywhere you intend on claiming as your own—your favorite brunch spot, bookstore, yoga studio. If He keeps coming into contact with your posse and their frosty smiles, eventually He'll get the message. Sure it's sneaky, but this is a Turf War. If a girl cannot knock back a few martinis in her favorite Saturday night restaurant without fear of bumping into Him, where can she relax?

Battling for Buddies

Getting dumped also means saying goodbye to His crowd. The custody battle over buddies is a cold, ugly reality of breaking up. This is
a time when you find out who your true friends really are—and the
ones who come out of the woodwork can surprise you. They aren't
the people who call with the perfunctory "I'm sorry." Or the faux
sympathetic "I just heard. You guys were so perfect together. Now tell
me everything!" No. The true friends are the ones who lend you their
Visa card to rent the moving van. They're the friends who call you
every evening for the following six weeks just to chat or to invite you
out for a walk. They're the neighbors, friends, or colleagues who cancel your appointments for you the morning after a Bittergirl Breakdown and don't remind you what you said and did the night before.
They're the friends who don't question why the hot young intern
from your firm answers your door in his boxers and who don't comment when he leaves your place on his ten-speed. They may not be
members of your team or even a BBGF, but they're friendships you
want to work at, not the ones you have to chase in hopes of insider
information on how He's coping.

As for His friends, it doesn't matter if you spent the last three New
Year's Eves with Mickey and Mimi and even sang at their wedding.
If they were His friends first, then His friends they will likely remain.
If Mimi calls to "see how you're doing," resist the urge to purge and
just give her a simple "I'll be okay." The less said the better. You don't
want your pathetic cries to come back and haunt you when you're
over Him and feeling great. And you certainly don't want Him
knowing that your shrink is avoiding your calls, that your dentist
phoned because she's worried about your last reaction to the laughing gas, and that your parish priest has sent around rotating groups
from the Ladies Church Auxiliary to check up on you. *Your* friends,

not His, are the lucky recipients of your 3 A.M. phone calls. When you're well and truly over Him, you can reassess your friendship with Mickey and Mimi.

Family Matters

The same goes for His family. They are blood. You are not. The rules of family engagement have changed. They're not your surrogate family even if they are your child's grandparents. It doesn't matter how close you were to them. Do not bad-mouth Him, and above all else remember the importance of Keeping Up Appearances. Stalking His brother or His mother will not provide enlightenment as to why He dumped you. Trust the bittergirls: If you must see them, keep your head high and let them wonder how He ever could have let you go.

The Exorcism

Reclaiming Your Space is another small gift you can give yourself simply by making it yours. You can sell that plasma screen television that took up half of your den; you can buy new sheets for your bed or change the bedroom around entirely. Just think, no more compromising where the couch goes or whether or not that painting by His sister gets hung. You can toss His stupid lacrosse trophies, reintroduce the throw pillows He thought were girlie, hang those old wicker baskets you used to collect pre-Him, paint the bathroom whatever color you feel like, and repaint it next week if the whim strikes you.

Once you've reclaimed your space you cannot let Him back in. Unless childcare duties involve Him being in your home, KEEP HIM OUT! Once He's been there to drop off your copy of *The Catcher in the Rye,* He'll permeate your environment. His presence will linger for weeks. He liked the vase of flowers on the mantelpiece, so now every time you look at the mantelpiece you'll think of Him. He thought the Modigliani should go on that wall. You'd thought that already but the next time He's there (and He will be when He comes back to you, right?) He's going to think you put it there because of Him.

Reclaiming Your Space won't bring Him back and it won't stop Him from being your first thought every morning, but at the very least it will eat up a few hours of your day if you're still in that BBRP phase when every day feels never-ending.

Isn't It Ironic?

So let's say you finally make it, fully dressed, out the door. You get as far as the corner coffee shop, where the cute couple with the matching lattes and the habit of feeding each other their *pain au chocolat* at the cash register is revolting enough to make you buy your java elsewhere. Heck, that extra six-block walk uphill is worth it to avoid them. But you can't avoid everyone, and Murphy's Law dictates that as soon as you get dumped, one of your close friends or family members is bound to get engaged or pregnant. In the bittergirl experience it's usually both.

The end of a relationship is a tough, lonely time. This is not a time to pull away from your friends, no matter how happy or perfect their lives may appear. Believe it or not, someday you're going to be over Him, but you'll never get another chance to see your best friend experience the birth of her first child or to help your sister with her wedding invitations. Of course the thought of picking up the phone to tell your friends Mark and Nicole that you and He won't be able to drive up to their cottage in their new SUV to see their renovations and their latest ultrasound is too painful to comprehend. But please, for your own sake, don't turn otherwise harmless onlookers into the bad guys. By being in the periphery of your life, your family and friends are merely the spectators in your breakup. They don't deserve to be cut out of your world simply because they're happy. Sure it's difficult watching other people living the life that was supposed to be yours, but you have no idea what fabulous future is waiting for you around the corner. The urge to hermit can be overwhelming, but by Renavigating Your Life you can make sure the life you have now is entirely yours. So He dumped you—don't let Him take your true friends with Him too.

Laughter and unexpected moments of joy come from the most surprising situations, not while you're on your second bag of junk food with an evening of sitcoms ahead of you. So while it may seem futile right now, trust us, get out there. We know you can do it. Go on. Embrace your life again. You're on your way, the bittergirl way.

bitteractivities

1. Pre-Him   Make a list of five things you used to do before you met Him. Vow to do one of them this week.

2. Me Without You   Who are you? Let it all out. Write until you can't think of anything else, then write some more.

I am the person who got dumped. . . .

I am the godmother of a beautiful child. . . .

I am the best daiquiri maker of all my friends. . . .

3. Things You Should Know   This is a chance to make a list of all the things you'd like to tell Him. Be brutal. Be honest. Then burn it.

Groceries are cheaper without you.

Your sister's a bitch.

I lied. You really can see your bald spot. . . .

4. Cashmere Revisited   Was there a certain outfit He didn't like? Wear it. A singer He couldn't stand? Turn up the volume. A food He didn't like? Make it for dinner. You get the idea. . . .

six

relationship mythology

OH SWEETIE, we know. Just when you think you're progressing steadily through the BBRP, you get hijacked. A big fat lonely moment swings through your world and you can't help but think back to the halcyon days of sunshine and roses when there wasn't a discordant note in the soundtrack of your life. You're flooded by sweet memories of Him. And before you know it, Relationship Mythology has commandeered your brain and you have no power to fight the legend of your love.

The Bittergirl Institute for Advanced Research on Dumping has uncovered some telltale signs that you've begun to rewrite the history of you and Him as a bliss-filled, extraordinary myth.

Happily Never After

Remember His smile? Remember His perfect white teeth and full, sensual lips? Don't you still love that picture of Him in the cable-knit sweater where He's smiling at you with such love you can actually see it in His eyes? Remember you were worried that you might not be as attracted to Him when He cut His long dark hair, but then He did and you loved Him even more? Remember when He brought you flowers for no reason, made you breakfast in bed, and read to you as you fell asleep? Who could forget how He'd recite Pablo Neruda in Spanish as He undressed you by candlelight or how He'd cry out "My beloved" in Swedish when He'd orgasm. Oh God, remember how He thanked you in His acceptance speech? There wasn't a dry eye in the house. Man, His motorcycle was sexy. All the little orphans loved it and begged for rides after His volunteer badminton lessons at the orphanage. He was so deep, so sensitive. Fragile almost. He was a mess after *Gandhi* and couldn't even speak after *Schindler's List.* And His parents! Tiff and Jon-Jon said you were like the daughter they never had. Oh, and His car with the leather interior and seat warmers and His songs that always managed to rhyme with your name in the chorus. Then there were the lazy Sundays in the park when you'd lie under the cherry blossoms together watching your kids play tag.

He was so wonderful. Flawed maybe; sure, who isn't? Get over this? Meet someone else? Look back at this someday without breaking into a sobbing mess? How? You'll always love Him. You'll never get over Him. There's nobody else like Him. Didn't you say that when you dedicated "One Fine Day" to Him on the radio the other night?

Yeah. Yeah. Yeah. We've said those words, felt those feelings, and most certainly cried those cries. Even the most jaded bittergirl goes through a phase of Relationship Mythology. But she wades through it, because that's all it is—MYTHOLOGY.

The *Little Oxford Dictionary* defines *mythology* as "a tale embodying especially an ancient popular belief or idea" and *myth* as "a fictitious person or thing." Now think about it: No matter how heartbroken you are, do you really want to spend what feeling you have left in your feeble little heart on an ancient belief or a fictitious person?

He peed in the shower—admit it. His ears looked goofy with short hair. Swedish orgasms? Please. He was quoting page 154 of last season's Ikea catalogue. You didn't fall asleep as He read to you; you fell asleep *because* He read to you. Motorcycles aren't sexy. Motorcycles are for assholes who never help their friends move or bring a case of beer to a party. Badminton with orphans? Yeah, they're the only ones who would let Him win. And didn't you want to scream when you had to leave the park early every single Sunday because the cherry blossoms triggered His asthma?

But you can't help it. In your current state you continue to create the legend that was once your other half. Day after day, week after week, you soothe your broken heart with the balm of Relationship Mythology. It's so much easier to remember what a Prince He was than try to imagine your future without Him. You spend hours shredding used tissues as you chastise yourself for not appreciating how He could mimic the call of a loon, how He always knew which way was west even in a strange city, how He knew all the chords to "Smoke on the Water" on the guitar. Why didn't you appreciate Him enough when He was here? You look at your home, your thighs, and your finances and you wonder, "What made Him leave?"

Honey, mythology is dangerous territory. Get caught there and you could get stuck. If you aren't careful, mythology will grab you like quicksand and you'll be so busy turning Him into someone He never was that you won't notice you're drowning. Getting dumped is hard enough to get over. He's probably hard to get over. Turning Him into a superhero or a saint is not going to help you recover from this any faster. TRUST US. The sooner you stop mythologizing Him, the sooner you'll be able to stop mythologizing the relationship.

We Were So Perfect

We've said it. We've heard it. Blah, blah, blah. . . . You guys were so perfect. Everybody said so. Other couples wished they could be you. You never fought. You didn't nag. The sex was great, for the most part. Why, sometimes you knew what He was going to say before He even said it! How many times did you stare in amazement as you finished each other's sentences? How many Friday nights did all the regulars beg you guys to do your special rendition of "Love Lifts Us Up Where We Belong" at karaoke? If that's not perfect, what is? Then there were the year-round walks by the lake where you'd stroll hand in hand and talk about your future. That time in France when He carried you through the field of . . . blah, blah, blah.

Sure. Maybe He brought you breakfast in bed, memorized your favorite sonnet, recited it at your wedding, and had no problem buying you tampons on His way home from work. We'd even believe you if you told us He held your hair back while you puked during last year's flu season. But He didn't do those things because it was the "perfect relationship." He did them because, chances are, you deserved them. Relationships thrive on give-and-take, and we have a hunch you did your share of the giving.

Endured Easter at the in-laws? Shivered through His mid-November soccer games? Gave birth to the twins, did His taxes, put the toilet seat down, cleaned the pubic hair out of the bathtub, let Him make monkey noises in the sack? The least He could do is bring you some damn flowers and rotate your tires once a year. That ain't mythology, baby. That's reciprocation.

Elana thought she and Jergen had had the perfect relationship. He was happiest staying home to spend romantic nights by the fire. He said she looked most beautiful in her favorite track pants and T-shirt. He loved working out at the gym with her. They did everything together. So when Jergen dumped her, Elana's world was crushed. But as she started to cut through the mythology, she had a rude awakening. She realized that all the things that had been so perfect about Jergen were just a cover for His insecurities and His desire to control every aspect of her life. If they stayed home most nights, nothing could divert her attention from Him; if she wore her track pants and T-shirt everywhere, no one else would see her fabulous body; if He worked out with her, He could make sure every gym member knew she was His girlfriend; they did everything together because that was the only way He could keep tabs on her.

Ladies, do you honestly believe there's such a thing as a Perfect Relationship? Come on! Have you ever noticed on television that when a relationship is described as "perfect" the husband has usually just killed the wife? You finished each other's sentences? That's not ESP. That's cutting each other off. Did you ever think that maybe He waited for you at the subway every night because He was a possessive control freak? Walks by the lake? What? Was He too cheap to spring for dinner now and then? Talked about the future? Well that's all it was, wasn't it? Talk. Talk. Talk. Talk. You knew what He was going to say before He said it? Why, because He was predictable? You never fought? Wow. That must have done wonders for your communication, not to mention your mounting resentments and issues with conflict.

Sure, mythologizing the perfection of your relationship might make you feel better for a short time. During this period you can lie on His side of the bed, the covers tucked tight around you, and reminisce about how fantastic you were together. You can keep your photos of Him on the wall and polish His hockey trophies. You can try to convince yourself that since the relationship was so perfect. *He has to come to His senses and realize what He's giving up!* You could lie in the bath and listen to "You Are an Obsession" and "It Must Have

Been Love" on repeat until you look like a prune, and you could make some of His favorite foods for when He changes His mind and comes back! This is almost acceptable behavior during the initial aftermath of the breakup, when you're still grieving your loss and figuring out how to cancel the dinner party you were meant to be hosting that weekend. If mythology gets you through the shock, so be it.

But staying trapped there is another issue entirely. It doesn't matter how wonderful you thought your relationship was or how He leapt over tall buildings with a single bound. It's over. It hurts. Turning the relationship into something it never was will not help you get over this any quicker.

Trust us. THERE IS NO SUCH THING AS THE PERFECT RELATIONSHIP. Whoever tells you otherwise is selling you a false bill of goods.

Justify, Justify His Love

One day, as you dust His beer stein collection with the sleeve of your pajamas, it hits you. You know why He dumped you! He has a terminal disease, something really awful. He probably got it from His sister, whose husband just finished that research assignment in the tropics. It's probably some brain-eating parasite or those flesh-eating worms that live in you until they kill you. Some infirmity so terrible He knows it would break your heart, and because He loves you so much He wants to spare you from His pain. So He retreated like the martyr that He is to go and get treatment. That's why He hasn't picked up when you call, and why His friends gave you those pitying stares when you showed up at their weekly poker game to drop off the odd sock you found under the bed that you thought He might need now that the weather is getting colder.

Or what if it isn't a rare disease? What if He witnessed a crime so terrible that He's had to go into hiding? Everybody's been talking about that graffiti on the back door of the bakery. The whole neighborhood is just going into decline! Maybe those hang-ups He was getting before The Incident were intimidation tactics from the criminals or pleas from the FBI to flee the country. Okay, the police probably would have called, but what does it matter at a time like this? Why didn't He tell you? Didn't He think you were strong enough to handle the truth? Did He think you wouldn't have gone into hiding with Him because you need to talk to your mother every day? Now He's alone and on the run with an incurable parasite roaming His brain, and here you are feeling sorry for yourself! You never knew what a true hero you were with!

When you're living in the land of Relationship Mythology it's so easy to misinterpret His current behavior. "I think He still loves me," you say. "I can tell by the way He looks at me, the things He . . . if things weren't so . . . well, just stuff." The bittergirls say: "Really? What stuff? What looks? Name one."

We bittergirls have seen too many mythologizers mistake pity for love, looks of concern for a magic connection, a common cold for a terminal illness. These are familiar blunders, but honey, we're here to stop you from sliding down that slippery slope. Unless He's spelling out His love for you letter by letter in large diamonds, with a hard copy of this declaration as backup, don't make His actions out to be anything more than what they are.

"But we still talk to each other better than anybody else and it's been two years since He left. He'll figure it out eventually." Okay, maybe you do talk. Maybe after years apart you still connect better than most couples who are still together. Maybe He's just a great conversationalist. Maybe it's easy to chat effortlessly when you aren't a part of each other's every day, when there's no obligation, no depending on each other, no sense of responsibility. It doesn't mean He wants to buy a dream home with you. The fact that you and He still make each other laugh doesn't mean He's coming back. His mechanic is funny, and He can talk politics with his contractor for hours. He's not sleeping with them either, is He?

Oh sweet, trusting bittergirl, you can make all the excuses in the world for Him. He just needs to work some stuff out, He's a spy, He's not good at putting His feelings into words, He needs to quit the firm and get the band back together, He wasn't nurtured enough as a child, He was in *Up with People!* The list is endless—we know, we've written it too. The thing is, the longer you wait for Him, the longer and more ridiculous that list of excuses becomes. Do yourself a favor: Write those justifications down because someday you'll look at them and laugh out loud. Remember, He left. And if all He has is a parasite crawling around in His body to show for it, He got off easy.

Burst That Bubble, Baby

Now to the outside eye it might look like you're moving on, like you're dealing with this abrupt change in your life. Maybe your walk is confident (you can thank the fuck-me boots for that). Your eyes sparkle and you have more social engagements than there are hours in the day. You're the hit of every party, the belle of the ball, the cat's pajamas. But if someone were to ask you what Sue served at her dinner party last week or what you wore to the gallery opening the other night, you'd be at a loss. Come to think of it, if anyone asked you what you had for lunch yesterday or what the punchline was to the joke you told this morning, you wouldn't have a clue. But if you were asked what you had on your hamburger that weekend you and He went skiing or what He thought of the second-round NHL draft pick from two years ago, you could answer without hesitation.

Oh dozy bittergirl! You've been sleepwalking through your life, haven't you? While going through the motions of your day it looks as though you're present and accounted for, but we know better. Remember, we've been in dreamland too. We know you're reliving every moment of your time together in your head. It's as though there's a movie projector in there and all you can see is the never-ending film of The Life That Used to Be Yours. Image after image, conversation after conversation plays on as you sit in that board meeting, listen to your new date's stories, or cycle around Timbuktu.

You tell yourself that if you'd known you'd be reliving those memories again and again and again, you'd have lived them fuller. You wouldn't have worried so much about the bills or your career. You would have looked into His eyes more, flirted while you did the dishes. And the relentless film continues as you stumble blindly through your day.

Deirdre confessed that "Apparently my best friend got married last spring. I was there but I don't remember it. I know I wore lavender and gave a great speech, but when the groom kissed the bride, I was with Erick at a cottage in the Laurentians on a creaky single bed naming our future children."

Lissi told us that "I've heard it was a mild winter but I wouldn't know. We were back in the old neighborhood looking for our first house."

He may not be by your side anymore, but you haven't really let Him leave. You write Him letters in your head. You read novels or watch films through His eyes. You have conversations about them in your mind. Well, that's safe, isn't it? As long as you're scripting the conversation between you and Mythology Man, He'll never disagree with you, He'll never sound stupid like the time He told you that Neil Diamond sang "A Reverend in Blue Jeans," He'll never complain about how long it's taking you to get ready, He'll never just mutter "Fine" when you ask Him about His day. He probably never wears that acrylic sweater you hate and He never slouches. Mythology Man never farts and always waits for you to orgasm before He does. He'll always be perfect in your screenplay.

Mallon was stopped at a red light when she saw her Mythology Man waiting to cross the street. At first she had to double-check that it was actually Him. He seemed shorter and He had no chin. In her months of daydreaming about Him, He was taller and had a chiseled jaw. Who was this mere mortal who had to wait at the crosswalk like everybody else? No, she wasn't over Him in an instant, but it did make her wonder about what other elements of her life she hadn't seen properly since her breakup with the chinless wonder.

When you sleepwalk through your life stuck in Relationship Mythology, you cease to move on. You remain trapped as the person you were in that relationship. However comforting those memories may be, you can't stay wrapped up in them. You're a different person from the one you were in the moments before The Incident. Since then your world has been turned upside down. Maybe you have to find a new place to live or figure out how your car insurance might change. Maybe you just have to get off the couch and wash your hair for the first time in a week. You have things to do. You have a life to live. You can't do that while you're back in the land of The Way We Were. The Way *We* Were doesn't matter. The Way *You* Are does.

But I Was So Happy

"But I was so happy," you say. Were you? Stopped sleeping in because He was a morning person? Stopped eating meat because He was a vegetarian? Didn't see so-and-so anymore because He didn't like her husband? Didn't order that last glass of wine because *He* didn't like losing control? Took up tennis, skiing, stamp collecting, or line dancing because that's what He liked? Hey, it's great to have hobbies in common, but not at the risk of losing your own identity.

Following her breakup with John, Kristen was amazed at how many little things she had changed in the years she'd been with Him. It's not as though He'd asked her to change, but without noticing, she was spending more time rock climbing than fly-fishing—the sport *she* loved—and was saving for a model of off-road Jeep that she didn't particularly want. When John told her He wasn't attracted to her personality anymore, she wasn't sure which personality He was referring to. In the months they had tried to make things work, Kristen worked more, slept less, and became a powerhouse in bed, walking the tightrope between who she thought she was and who she imagined John wanted her to be. At home alone one morning in her pajamas, drinking tea and chatting long distance to a friend, she had an epiphany. This was who she was—a loyal friend who loved to laugh, a homebody who liked to putter and to spend hours with the weekend papers. John was the adrenaline junkie; she wasn't. When He eventually left to seek another thrill, she scaled her own mountain and reinvented her mythology.

Don't let Relationship Mythology skew your vision. Despite what you might feel right now, He wasn't purely responsible for your past happiness. Believe it or not, you had a whole lot to do with it.

The bittergirls were horrified to hear the saga of their old friend Pippa. Upon returning home after a sun-soaked year in Bali, her boyfriend Felix, who had told her all along that He "couldn't commit," finally didn't commit. Back home, single and heartbroken, Pippa thought her breakup meant the end of her global adventures. No Felix meant no travel. Nothing could ever compare to the blissful travel romance they'd had. What was the point of Costa Rica without Him? Night after night she'd sit weeping on her sister's couch, mourning the loss of her life as she knew it. Then, as an early birthday gift (and to get Pippa's tear-soaked ass off her couch, we suspect), her sister bought her Spanish lessons. Once a week Pippa would trudge through the snow-covered streets to slowly reembrace her life. As she learned to converse with her classmates, they shared their love of travel, they sought out a tiny Costa Rican restaurant, they listened to Spanish music. She began to take guitar lessons from one of them. One day while standing in a line to have her passport updated she realized with a jolt that she hadn't thought about Felix in days. And what's more, she felt happy.

Maybe If . . . The Fault Line

Ooooh, but there is a nasty sense of betrayal that comes with Relationship Mythology. As we travel the incessant cycle of "but we were so good together" and "I was so happy," we inevitably ask ourselves the question: If it was so good, why didn't it work?

Honey, as long as He and the relationship were perfect you'll end up blaming yourself for the breakup. It's so easy to chastise yourself for not doing enough, not being enough, and not seeing it coming. You can spend countless hours wondering where it went wrong or how you screwed it up. Maybe if your face was oval? Maybe if you'd let Him alphabetize your CDs? Maybe if you hadn't cut your hair or gone back to school? Maybe if you *had* had oral sex that week you had your wisdom teeth out?

When mythologizing the relationship, if you don't blame yourself, you might blame the universe for keeping the two of you apart. Maybe if His boss hadn't offered Him that promotion He wouldn't have gone on that business trip and He wouldn't have met Callie and things would have been fine. You begin to wonder if you did something horrendous in a past life that's coming back to haunt you. That's right; it's the karma police tearing Him from you because of that jug of wine you stole when you were a slave in ancient Egypt!

Maybe if your cousin hadn't asked about His golf handicap last Thanksgiving? Maybe if people would have stopped asking when He was going to propose? Maybe if the national deficit was lower?

Sugar, all the maybe-ifs in the world and all the blaming other people still won't help. If only there was a magic answer that would help it all make sense. That's one of the most difficult parts of getting dumped. Not knowing why. When you're looking for answers, searching for reasons why your life has suddenly become the stuff of Greek tragedy, the need to know WHY becomes frantic. But even if He gave you a different reason every week for the next ten years, the answer would never be satisfactory. It doesn't matter how He says it or why He did it, it won't make it any easier. Heartbreak is heartbreak and it hurts like hell.

By focusing on all the maybe-ifs, Robyn found herself trapped in the past world of her and Paolo. She analyzed each moment of the months leading up to The Incident. Maybe if they had taken that vacation in February instead of May. Maybe if she hadn't loved the rain. Maybe if she hadn't been allergic to peanuts. She drew up different outcomes for their relationship based on certain choices she'd made. After exhausting every possible maybe-if, she came to a heartbreaking conclusion: Even if she could go back and change these moments, the ending would still be the same. Paolo dumped her.

The World Outside Your Window

Now, it's known worldwide that the bittergirls are NOT about getting over one man in the hopes of meeting another. However, we bittergirls are a fabulous bunch and we cannot help it if other men find us irresistible, can we? This brings us back to the dangers of Relationship Mythology. If you're still wrapped in that cocoon of memories, then honey, you can't see the world full of great men who are still out there. You've been so hypnotized by the one who's done you wrong that you might just miss the one who almost got away.

When Georgia's ex left her with a mortgage comparable to the debt of a Third World country, she knew she'd have to find somewhere smaller and cheaper to live. She found solace in a quaint old house in dire need of some TLC. Georgia threw herself into her fixer-upper and relived the entire relationship in her head as she scraped, sanded, and learned all about drill bits. She was so busy editing the story of her "perfect relationship" that she almost missed the happy ending standing in her kitchen every day: her handyman. There's a reason he took so long building the cabinets. And lucky for Georgia, eventually she noticed the size of his toolbelt.

The Myth of You

We're not saying turn Him into a bad guy and we're not saying wipe out all your memories. We're saying don't get stuck in those memories and don't make them better than they were. Relationship Mythology is seductive. Stay lost in the "what was" and you'll lose what's left of the rest of your life. Honey, if there's one thing the bittergirls know from experience, it's that while you're barricading yourself away, your great big juicy life is marching right past your window.

So He wasn't perfect. But maybe He was pretty fantastic in your eyes. Was there *any* area of the relationship that was lacking? What did you settle for? Was there anything that you just put up with or deep down weren't too happy with? Ask yourself why you put up with it. How much did you compromise in the name of love? Check out Chapter 7: "Warning Signs."

Here's a dare. Write a list of what you feel you lost when you lost Him. It can be anything from losing your house to losing the permission to be afraid of the dark. You might have lost the feeling of being loved or you may have lost the nicknames you had for each other. You may have lost the barbeque, the bookshelves, and your private jokes. But here's what you didn't lose—YOURSELF. Maybe your Kernel has gone AWOL but you'll get it back. The relationship is over. You aren't. It's time to start mythologizing yourself.

There are many paths into the land of Relationship Mythology, but the only road out is to be a true bittergirl and keep moving forward. If you're so busy living in the past and the world of make-believe, then who's living your fabulous reality? So go ahead, stay up all night, finish that trashy novel, and then sleep in. Put away the pearls and slap on those sequins. Pick up that tennis racket and get those Bay City Rollers CDs back in your collection. Mythologize the you that you are today, not the you you were with Him.

Meanwhile, think long and hard about this. If it was so great, why isn't He still here?

♈ bitteractivities

1. Maybe If I'd . . .   Stop punishing yourself! You're not to blame for this breakup (unless you slept with His best friend or a member of His family, or did something illegal). But no matter what you do, you'll still likely question whether things would be different if you hadn't snorted when you laughed or if you'd been able to run three miles instead of just five. So just to get it all out of your system, fill in the following sentence until there's nothing left for you to write.

Maybe if I'd _____ He wouldn't have left me.

Trust us, the maybe-ifs will become so ridiculous you'll realize there's nothing you could have done. If He left, He left. The Bittergirl Institute for Advanced Research on Dumping has heard them all. Here are some of the more memorable ones:

Maybe if I'd let Him paint in the bedroom.

Maybe if I'd worn more makeup.

Maybe if I'd had skinnier legs.

Maybe if I'd tried to understand football.

Maybe if I'd stayed up late.

Maybe if I'd worn plum eye shadow instead of beige.

Maybe if I'd said I didn't want children.

Maybe if I'd watched more hockey.

Maybe if I'd had better underwear.

Maybe if I'd walked on the north side of the street.

Maybe if I'd worked out more.

Maybe if I'd let Him read at the table.

Maybe if I hadn't talked to my mother so much.

Maybe if I'd let Him pick the movies.

Maybe if I'd just been better.

2. Habitual Annoyances   Make Him a Superhero of His bad habits. How can you glorify The Aimless Wonder or The Superhero of Pee on the Bathroom Floor? Tape it to your fridge, your bathroom cabinet, His side of the bed.

3. Coupling   Make a list of all the things you miss doing together. Who's to say you can't do them on your own? This may sting, but ask yourself: Do you miss Him or do you miss being part of a couple?

4. Mythologize Yourself   Imagine that you just broke up with someone and they were spending their days mythologizing *you*. What would they say? How would they describe you?

seven

warning signs

Phew, what a relief! Now you can admit that your relationship wasn't perfect. You've demythologized the legend of Him and purged all the maybe-ifs out of your system. You're starting to get reacquainted with the fabulousness of your soul. Well, that's just the tip of your iceberg, honey. It's now the time in the BBRP when you're strong enough to consider some of those things you might have overlooked as you traveled the bumpy road to bittergirldom.

If you were asked to rewrite the true story of your relationship, we bittergirls are willing to bet you had a couple of inklings that a storm was looming. Sweetie, these inklings were the little hints that in some way or other foreshadowed The Incident: They were the Warning Signs.

In supermarket lines, waiting rooms, train stations, and traffic jams around the world, bittergirls mentally play Identify the Warning Sign, thereby passing time while maintaining the calm, poised bittergirl persona. However, before you can play, you must be able to identify a Warning Sign. For example, you were married for eleven years but He never gave you His cell number? That's a Warning Sign. He cried at Céline Dion songs? Warning Sign. Wouldn't let you eat in

His car? Gave you shoelaces for your birthday? Bought you out-of-season vegetables for the entire Twelve Days of Christmas? Warning Sign, Warning Sign, Warning Sign.

The bittergirls believe that no breakup has ever come completely out of the blue. THERE ARE ALWAYS WARNING SIGNS. The beauty in identifying the Warning Sign is that once you do, the next time you'll spot it a mile away. Remember what the American philosopher George Santayana said: "Those who forget the past are condemned to repeat it." Okay, so maybe he wasn't referring to getting dumped, but the same rules apply. Forget the Warning Signs and you could once again find yourself wiping your new boy's tear-soaked eyes to the theme song from *Titanic* faster than you can spell *F-R-E-A-K!*

In the immediacy of a breakup when everything is fresh and raw, the Warning Sign game may cause unprovoked moments of fury. "How could I have been so blind?" "How could I have missed that?!" Luckily the bittergirls are here to remind you that you were in a relationship, not the Police Academy, so stop smacking yourself with that stiletto. (When you feel better you might want to wear it once more—and that heel is no good to you broken!) No, the purpose in identifying the Warning Signs is not to chastise yourself; it's so that they NEVER HAPPEN AGAIN.

When you reexamine the terrain of your relationship, chances are He gave you plenty of warning that He was on the way out. You just weren't trained to pick up on or deal with the not-so-subtle clues. That's why the bittergirls are here. The Bittergirl Institute for Advanced Research on Dumping has spent years studying Warning Signs. It has distinguished four main avoidance styles women typically use to sidestep the issues, and five of the most common behavioral Warning Signs exhibited by men.

Top Four Avoidance Styles
Adopted by Women

Turning a Blind Eye

At some point in the relationship you recognize at least a couple of Warning Signs, but you're too wrapped up in making things work and so push those nasty thoughts aside. Who are you to be so judgmental? It's not as though you're all that perfect, you tell yourself. Relax; you aren't with Him to change Him. So He scratches His balls in public. What guy doesn't? He says three Hail Mary's on His knees while wearing your panties? Moans your mother's name in His sleep? You don't want to dwell on the Warning Sign, so you simply ignore it. And don't be fooled. Warning Signs can happen on a first date or after years of being in a fabulous relationship.

Kate will never forget the Warning Sign she ignored. After months of intense flirting with a bad-boy teammate in her soccer league, they ended up back at His place one night. As they headed into the bedroom she noticed Him kick what looked suspiciously like a used sex towel under the bed. With one flick of a light switch the room was filled with the glow of a disco ball and the sounds of "Let's Get It On." Ignoring her instinct, they got it on until the moment He looked down at her and said, "Baby, have I got a load for you." If it looks like a porno and sounds like a porno, you should get paid to be in the porno. Warning Sign.

Brenda and Ted worked together in the same department for the last year of their relationship. For months it bugged Brenda that at the office Ted wouldn't acknowledge they were a couple. But He was the consummate professional, and since things were so great when they were away from work Brenda turned a blind eye to it. Returning to the office late one night after a long meeting off-site, she walked into the photocopy room to find her cubicle mate, Rebecca, and her very own Ted necking furiously on the Xerox machine. Consummate professional indeed. Warning Sign.

bittergirlspeak

Honey, if there's one lesson you can learn, it's to never ignore your instincts! If you have that niggling feeling that it's a sex towel, it probably is. Unless you and your guy are working a life-threatening undercover sting operation, secrecy is never okay. When we turn a blind eye to the notion that something's wrong, it's often because we don't want to accept the reality that lies behind it. But baby, that reality won't go away, and sooner or later it's going to catch up with you.

Living the Dream

You've seen all the films, so you know that life is one big fairy-tale romance. You know how to play your part. You have the lines memorized, the facial expressions down pat. Of course, the movies have taught us to ignore Warning Signs. How many stupid teenage babysitters does it take to figure out that the noise on the other side of the door is the killer?

In the movies, if she ditches her poodle skirt and gets a perm and some leather, He'll show up at the fair in a letterman sweater! Our heroine never gives up on the bad boy, and sure enough He always comes riding back into town on His Harley, or takes Baby out of the corner, or picks her up off the factory floor without getting His shiny white uniform dirty, or climbs up her fire escape and while His limo waits curbside He tells her He doesn't care if she's a hooker. Sometimes He even does penance by coaching an inner-city kids' football team, or His best friend has to plummet to his death in a plane crash going Mach 5. Whatever. The point is, He changes. Yeah, right. What changes in Hollywood is the *ending*, honey.

Take the stage play *Sexual Perversity in Chicago*. They meet, fall in love, move in together, He can't take it, He leaves. The end. When they made it into a movie they called it *About Last Night*. . . . They meet, fall in love, move in together, He can't take it, He leaves. But then He figures it all out, He comes back, and they walk off into the sunset toward the land of happily ever after. Sure they do.

Even our childhood fairy tales teach us to ignore Warning Signs. If Cinderella had to sneak into the ball in a borrowed outfit, is she really going to be comfortable spending the rest of her life with His crowd? Hello? Princess Diana? If Snow White had to get a husband by cooking and cleaning up for seven little men, is her Prince going to take her seriously when she says she wants to go back to school? And what about Belle? Isn't it not just dangerous but stupid to move in with a beast? If it looks like a beast and acts like a beast, what are the chances it's really a Prince? Come on, girls, if you keep on kissing toads, perhaps the problem lies with you and not the frog. As embarrassing as it may be, at some point we have to take a long look at ourselves and our choices. Altering our own behavior (for the better) is much healthier than trying to change somebody else's.

Rhonda and Parker had the fairy-tale relationship. They met at university when His fraternity was hosting a dinner for her sorority. They had the fairy-tale wedding, bought the fairy-tale house in the fairy-tale neighborhood, and were planning to have three fairy-tale children. Then Rhonda landed a kick-ass job that was the envy of their entire circle of friends. And that's where the fairy tale took a nasty turn. In Parker's fairy tale, the Mommy Bear never made more than the Daddy Bear and if she did, the story had a very unhappy ending. He never even congratulated Rhonda on her achievement. Parker's ego couldn't hack the fact that she was more successful than He in her career, so He set out to destroy her personal happiness. After months of giving her the silent treatment and hinting at an affair, Parker finally walked out, leaving Rhonda alone in their once-perfect house in their once-perfect neighborhood. Luckily she didn't wait a hundred years for the next Prince to kiss her. Rhonda sold the house, moved into a funky renovated flat, and reveled in her new fairy tale of freedom.

bittergirlspeak

Remember, the only constant in fairy tales, Hollywood movies, and real-life relationships is that at some point they all come to an end. Some end more unhappily than others, but if you read the plot correctly you can usually figure out the outcome of the story before the back of the hardcover is slammed down on your heart.

The Change Challenge

All the Warning Signs are laid out for you to see. But you decide that these aren't signs at all; they're pleas for help! He wants you to help Him! When He says He doesn't want children, you just know you'll change His mind. Once He meets your goddaughter Gabriella, He'll thank you for helping Him see the light. When He jokes that He can't even spell *monogamy*, you line up the Scrabble tiles *M-O-N-O-G-A-M-Y* on His bedside table and promise to help Him with that. You don't like any of His friends or their Harley-Davidson tattoos. You're not judgmental. You just know that deep down He'd be happier hanging out with Bobby and Fred at the country club sipping Pimms in His tennis whites. When He tells you with pride that His pals call Him "Extra Large," you honestly believe that in time His appreciation for Japanese films will outweigh His obsession with genitalia.

You've been snowed by the illusion that love has the power to change Him, whether He wants to change or not. In fact, you believe, He *needs* you to change Him. While in rare instances this has been known to happen, The Bittergirl Institute for Advanced Research on Dumping warns that setting out to change somebody is a guarantee for disaster.

Eleanor was head over heels for Graham. He was a successful contractor who ran His own business, loved His truck, and enjoyed weekends at the cottage. She had a great job in Finance and loved to spend her money on Him. She bought Graham a whole new wardrobe from J. Crew, refurnished His apartment with a minimalist eye, and even splurged on a brand-new SUV for His birthday. Nothing was too good for precious Graham. After a devastating breakup, she saw Him driving around in a beat-up old pickup wearing one of His old plaid shirts. What's that saying? "You can lead a horse to water but you can't make it wear J. Crew."

👄 bittergirlspeak

When you hear yourself describe His endearing traits, are they things you intend to teach Him? Warning Sign. When you go into a relationship to change Him, you've pretty much stamped the best-before date on it before you've even slept together. Nobody wants to be your class project. That's what those television makeover shows are for. If you're looking at a lump of coal, it's not going to become a diamond overnight no matter how much you want it to.

Excuses, Excuses

The two of you are SO happy. Sure, there might have been a couple of biggie Warning Signs thrown your way, but you make a conscious choice not to let them faze you. You come up with reasons for His outrageous, off-kilter, or unacceptable behavior and you broadcast them to anyone in earshot. Like the Tuesday He stumbled home at 5 A.M. with lipstick stains around His collar after a night out with the boys. You know full well how much those boys need to let off some steam. They work so hard. So what if they went to a strip club, got a little silly, and Blair stole a dancer's lipstick and tried to get all the guys in trouble with their gals? You and the girls aren't exactly pure as the driven snow, are you?

No matter how shameful, bizarre, shocking, hurtful, or offensive His actions may be, your imagination works at full throttle to explain away every single sign. He won't come with you to your best friend's engagement party because He's depressed, He's always out drinking because He's really not happy in His job, He keeps the door of His home office locked because He doesn't want the kids messing up His desk, He's not in the mood for sex because He's not happy with His body. The list goes on. After all, isn't it your duty as a committed, loving partner to make allowances for your man? You believe these excuses you're making for Him are simply a gal's way of showing empathy and compassion. And you have to say them out loud for other people to hear because that will somehow make them more real.

When Tristan gave Shoana a facial before their first anniversary dinner, she suspected something was wrong. Instead of heeding the Warning Sign, she decided that He was concerned about skin care because He had suffered such horrible acne in His teens. When Tristan came out of the closet four months later, deep, deep down Shoana had to admit she shouldn't have been surprised.

💋 bittergirlspeak

WAKE UP! You may think you're being compassionate and understanding, but underneath you're desperate and delusional. Blinded by love, you could justify just about anything. You could convince yourself that Hannibal Lecter, Dr. Christian Szell in *Marathon Man,* and Mussolini are all cute, innocent, loving men. Honey, the moment you start making excuses for Him, put the brakes on, reapply your lipstick, and excuse yourself from the relationship.

Now that you've figured out which avoidance style you tend to favor, it's time to fix your eyes on the Warning Signs most often cited in breakup behavior studies.

Five Most Common Warning Signs Exhibited by Men

Commitment Phobia

The loudest and by far the most common Warning Sign comes with just three little words. Oh, the seduction, the intoxication, just the mere mention of them and we're instantly transported to another universe—"I Can't Commit."

Girls, why do we hear that as a challenge instead of a Warning? The words are no sooner out of His mouth and we're off, straight into avoidance style number three, telling anybody who'll listen that "I'll be the one who changes Him." With the proper amount of love and caring you'll tame the demons, put Humpty-Dumpty back together again, help Him forget His crappy childhood, show Him it's not too late to play lead guitar with Aerosmith. You'll take care of Him, mother Him, be His nanny, His coach, His best friend, you'll love Him so much better than anyone else ever has that He'll have to commit to you. Ladies, He's a guy, not a puppy. No amount of training will make Him stay. If He wants to stay, He will. If He doesn't, let Him go pee against someone else's fire hydrant.

Listen carefully when He says "I can't commit." What He's really saying is *"I can't commit."*

Arielle still marvels at her brush with commitment-phobic Ramblin' Man. "I remember He kissed me, looked deep into my eyes, and said 'Don't fall in love with me babe, I'm trouble. There's a little girl in Texas who doesn't know her Daddy.' I wanted to burst out laughing it was so cheesy, but it was almost a dare, so what did I do? Fell in love with Him of course. And He broke my heart."

💋 bittergirlspeak

If a guy tells you He's not ready for a commitment, He knows He'll only hurt you, He doesn't like to be tied down, or He's not ready for anything serious, BELIEVE HIM. He's not playing games or challenging your relationship ability; He's warning you not to get involved.

Ex-Land

You can tell a lot about a guy by the way He talks about His past relationships. Was He always the one to end things? How many times has He been married? Has He ever been dumped? Been unfaithful? Left anyone at the altar? Does He have more than one stalker? Does He talk constantly about His ex? He claims He's over His last girlfriend but people keep on mistaking you for her. He breaks into sobs when He hears "their song." He makes you sleep on "her" side of the bed. He introduces you to her as His "friend" when you bump into her on the street. He makes you duck when you drive past her new place. Doesn't let you answer His telephone. Says they're not together anymore but still keeps all His stuff at her place and His voice is still on their machine. Is she still the beneficiary on His life insurance policy? Is His weekly newspaper column or current art exhibit about their breakup? Is her moisturizer still in the medicine cabinet? Does He bail on your best friend's birthday because He has to help her move, change a flat tire, look for her cat? Warning Sign. Warning Sign. Warning Sign.

Conversely, does He say cruel things about His exes? Does He make disparaging remarks about her or her girlfriends? Does He talk about how lousy she was in bed? How she nagged? How she demanded too much child support? How she hated all His buddies from His Monday, Wednesday, and Friday night bowling league? What a prude she was about Internet porn? How she complained when He gambled? Is He always the victim in His stories? Remember, if He trashes His exes, chances are He'll trash you too one day.

Tara was ecstatic when Solomon asked her out. He suggested she come to His Thursday night comedy gig and they'd go out for a late dinner. Tara didn't want to show up at the club by herself so she invited a whole bunch of friends along to see His stand-up routine. She was so excited to show off her new boyfriend-to-be. The excitement was short-lived. Solomon began the act by dedicating it to His ex-girlfriend Sandy. For the next hour He covered every intimate detail of their relationship, what a loser He was without her, and what a bitch of a beauty she was. Tara was mortified and her friends squirmed uncomfortably in their seats. Needless to say, the night ended abruptly after His act.

Amy met Jason at a party and they had an immediate connection. He invited Her over for dinner the following week and their first date lasted forty-eight hours. They were instantly a couple. Everything about Him was intense. She was swept up in the romance of it all. Three weeks into their relationship He gave her a letter He'd written the day she was first coming over for dinner. In it Jason wrote that He had a feeling she'd be the one to restore His faith in love, in life, in humanity. He'd been so hurt by His ex that He'd stopped believing in love. He hoped Amy would change that. At the time Amy thought it was so sweet. Eight months later when Jason left her to go back to His ex, Amy burned the letter. Apparently by teaching Him to love again, Amy had led Him right back to loving His old girlfriend.

👄 bittergirlspeak

It's so tempting to make excuses for the Man living in the land of Ex. After all, you say, the only way to get over someone old is to find someone new. Why shouldn't you be the one to heal His broken heart, to restore His faith in love, to make Him see that women aren't all the same? Doll, that's what shrinks are for. Send Him to a therapist, and if He comes back to you He's yours; if not, He was never meant to be.

His-Story

He seems so together. He's thirty-eight. He drives a sexy car, has a fantastic career—but He's still living at home while He saves for a house? Warning Sign. When He gets mad, is His first instinct to reach for His belt? Warning Sign. What kind of relationship do His parents have? What was His childhood like? Did His brother lock Him in the closet for hours when His parents went out? Did His mother coddle Him so much that He didn't ride the bus alone until He was fifteen? If He has kids of His own, what's His relationship with them like? How does He treat yours? The Bittergirl Institute for Advanced Research on Dumping often points to family history as a leading factor in a man's ability to form successful relationships. And believe the bittergirls, we've seen enough evidence to prove it.

Sam was stunned when her boyfriend Tony became resentful of the time she spent with her kids. When she realized that He wanted a mommy more than a lover, she chalked it up to experience and didn't charge Him for the six months of babysitting.

After a series of romances with damaged Bad Boys, bittergirl

Kathryn thought she'd struck gold when she met Isaac. Isaac was from a stable family and didn't have a single negative thing to say about any of His exes. Ah, Isaac. His parents had been together for forty years and never spoke a cross word to each other. Isaac adored His folks and they in turn adored Isaac and Kathryn. It wasn't until their first big conflict that Kathryn realized there were problems. Since Isaac grew up in a house where nobody ever argued, He had no idea how to do it. While Kathryn ranted and raved and tried to get to the root of any problem, Isaac turned into a Stepford wife, refusing to show emotion of any sort. Before long she realized why He never discussed His exes. As soon as any of them had shown signs of anger, imperfection, or human error, He left them and wiped the memory board clean. Oh Isaac, real life is standing hand in hand knee-deep in conflict, ready to take on the world. Give us a guy who loves a good argument over a mannequin any day.

👄 bittergirlspeak

Although we hate to admit it, sometimes there's a seed of truth in the notion that we seek to replicate the family life we grew up with. Although His history may make sense of His current behavior, acknowledge the Warning Signs, raise your martini glass, and repeat after us: *"It's over. I can't change His past to fix our future."*

Serial Cheater

We're continually stunned by those bittergirls who claim to be shocked when the man *they* stole off someone else leaves them for a newer model. We remember the story of Mindy, personal secretary of Mr. CEO. Sure, she didn't *mean* to break up His twenty-five-year marriage. Yes, she did go to private school with His youngest daugh-

ter. And wow, who wouldn't want to summer up at the lake and winter in St. Bart's? But come on, Mindy. Are you stupid? You went to
St. Bart's with the four-year-old twins, the baby, and the nanny who
can't speak English and you left Him alone in the city with His new
executive assistant?

💋 bittergirlspeak

Sweetheart, once a cheater always a cheater. What did you think? A few
rounds with you and suddenly He's St. Francis of Assisi? Please. Not
only is it called non-bittergirl behavior, it's also called karma. Now wipe
your eyes and go volunteer at a soup kitchen. And stop touching things
that aren't yours, like other people's husbands.

I Don't Wanna Grow Up

He lives in a stunning Victorian and every room is spectacularly fur-
nished except for His bedroom. It holds a futon and an Ikea bookshelf with two shelves missing. It's piled high with magazines and
there are calendar girls plastered all over the walls. He even has an
old traffic light in the corner that continually turns red, green,
amber, red. . . . Is that really a puke stain by your head on His futon?
Eek, it's a frat boy trapped in the body of an investment banker.
Double Warning Sign.

Marianna spent years mooning over Franklin the screenwriter. He was
so perfect, so creative, so dedicated. He spent half His year in her town,
following His muse, half the year back in upstate New York looking
after His aging mother. What dedication. What devotion. What love
for family—so admirable in this day and age. Oh, He wanted to move
in with her and care for the children with her; He loved those kids. He
couldn't have been more devoted to them if He were their real father.

But He had other obligations before Marianna and her family, and she admired Him for that. Then when His mother died He still didn't move in. He had promised His mother He would take care of her house after she'd gone.

👄 bittergirlspeak

Come on, Marianna, wake up and smell the coffee. Franklin had three other siblings who weren't giving up their lives and adult ambitions for Mom. Could it be that, hmm, maybe Franklin just didn't want to grow up and live with Marianna and the kids? Could that be too much of a shock to the system for a man who still lived six months of the year with Mommy at the age of forty-eight? Oh yeah, He was "looking after Mom," but all it meant was that well into midlife He'd never owned or rented property in His own name, Mom paid all the bills, and six nights out of seven she was making Him His childhood favorites for dinner. Sure He spent half His year with Marianna and the kids, but looky there, Marianna was feeding Him and paying the bills and all Franklin had to do was love the kids and hang with them. Not so hard when you're the same mental age as a teenage babysitter. So when Mom finally kicked the bucket, the bittergirls weren't surprised when Franklin found Himself a twenty-two-year-old unencumbered by adult obligations and dumped Marianna and the kids faster than you can say "Are you a grown-up?"

The bittergirls know that you're a big grown-up girl. Listen to the Warning Signs because chances are if He's behaving like a baby, He is a baby. Applying the laws of inertia, He'll want to stay one. Why not? You can always find someone to baby you. Just make sure it's not you who's doing the babying. 'Cause we suspect that what you really want is a big grown-up man. You don't deserve anything less.

* * *

Some Warning Signs are more obvious than others. When The Bittergirl Institute for Advanced Research on Dumping came out with the top five behavioral Warning Signs, they were quick to concede that there are countless more. Here are a few of the more blatant ones we've seen.

blatant warning signs

1. When He locks you in His van and plays "Suspicious Minds."

2. You met Him while visting your uncle in jail.

3. When asked how long you've been together He says six months as you say two years.

4. When He looks at you over the candlelit table and says "So how about a little of the old 69?" He isn't talking vintages.

5. When He tells you to direct your conversation to Mr. Happy, The Python, or Little Dave because He doesn't feel like talking, and worse yet, when He talks to Mr. Grumpy, The Champ, or Hot Rod because He doesn't want to talk to you.

6. When He asks you to iron His white hood with the eye holes.

7. He says He loves you but needs to live on the other side of the park from you and your eleven adopted children.

8. Worried about those track marks?

9. When He shows you the hole He made in the wall with his fist.

10. When you come home from work and He's lying in the bathtub fully clothed.

11. When He tells you He's exploring His sexuality by sleeping with your brother.

12. He tells you you're on Engagement Probation. If you pass the three-month test, He'll propose to you.

Warning Sign, Warning Sign, Warning Sign!

You know, there's a reason the phrase "men's intuition" doesn't exist. To balance the pain of childbirth, God gave us women's intuition. You know, that little voice that says "Maybe it *is* a little strange that I can't call Him on Tuesdays, Thursdays, and Saturdays." In our experience, if He locks the door to the den and spends hours with the shredder, He's either a criminal or He's having an affair. Maybe both. If the family budget is out of whack, He has hot chocolate every morning with the new Swedish swimsuit model across the hall, He's working out constantly and never wants to have sex with you—He could be planning your surprise fortieth, but then again . . . what does your intuition say?

One of our favorite bittergirl stories is about Emily, who suspected her husband was cheating. When He told her He had "another damn weekend conference" out of town, she helped Him pack, kissed Him goodbye at the door, and cooed lovingly how much she'd miss Him. The second His Rolls-Royce was out of the driveway she bolted into the den, emptied His precious shredder, and spent the next forty-eight hours painstakingly taping the evidence of His infidelity back together. Piece by piece she discovered hotel receipts, diamond bracelet bills, dinners for two at restaurants she'd never been to, and the paper trail of exactly where He was stashing hoards of extra cash! With her freshly photocopied evidence and her gut instinct intact, she walked away with half His fortune and the knowledge that she'd salvaged a part of her wounded pride.

Another bittergirl confesses that "I had a feeling my boyfriend might be connected to the mob. Like He never actually said 'There's something I have to tell you' or anything like that; it was just little things. He never had a bank account. The entire time we were together He was paid in cash for jobs He wouldn't talk about. We could never go over the border to those discount malls because He didn't have a passport. There were other things too, like instead of going out to dinner He'd spend the evening coaching me in ways to avoid police interrogations. Then the bar I worked at blew up the day He left town without saying goodbye. Something in my gut just said 'There's something going on here,' but I didn't listen. I mean, He wasn't the worst guy I'd ever dated."

Now beware, girls, there are as many subtle Warning Signs as there are men. Those quiet yet horrific moments when it dawns on you that He just doesn't love you anymore. They may be less humiliating than finding Him in the pantry naked on all fours with the au pair, but they're no less painful.

Cherie gauged how her man felt about her by calling it a "John Hannah" Warning Sign. "In the movie *Sliding Doors* there's a scene where Gwyneth Paltrow's character is across a crowded table; she's laughing and chatting and John Hannah's character just watches her with such a combination of tenderness and awe. It took my breath away because it was such a beautiful intimate moment and because I realized that my ex used to look at me like that. And He hadn't looked at me like that for a very long time. Looking back now, in that instant I knew we were over. It took months for the relationship to end, but at least I know I deserve a John Hannah moment. I'll have it again someday."

subtle warning signs

1. He doesn't bring you flowers.
2. He doesn't sing you love songs.

3. He hardly talks to you anymore when you come through the door at the end of the day.

4. You're playing Scrabble and He uses the letters L, O, V, and E to spell VOLE.

5. He orders you Chardonnay when you've always been a Sauvignon Blanc girl.

6. He picks you up an Oh Henry but you're allergic to nuts.

7. He buys cologne for Himself for the first time in your relationship.

8. He starts to tell you about a movie that you saw together.

9. You find His acceptance letter to a master's program in India that you didn't know He'd applied to.

10. His sister asks you what you're going to do when He takes that month-long solo hike in the Yukon.

Strange as it may seem while you're knee-deep in heartbreak hell, you probably had a few Warning Sign moments of your own. You know, those little voices whispering that maybe you were a little bored from time to time, that maybe you didn't just imagine the attraction between you and Junior's pediatrician? Maybe some nights you lay awake listening to Him snoring and thought about smothering Him. Maybe you even planned your funeral outfit. But you didn't do anything about it because you loved Him, you took your commitment seriously, you hadn't shaved your legs the day Dr. Dave made his move, or you were afraid that a women's prison isn't as much fun as it looks in *Chicago*. You had your own Warning Signs; you just didn't act on them.

Perhaps you suspected He had one foot out the door, but instead of bolting and beating Him to it you opted to stay and fight for the relationship. So you ignored the instinct that whispered "Run. Don't Walk." Well good for you for putting up the fight. Chalk it up to experience and remember what that twisted, knowing feeling in your gut feels like. Take the wisdom and move on.

If you keep a journal, go and take a look through some of your old entries. While you may not have proclaimed your misery in black and white, you may be surprised at the clues you find there. One bittergirl told us how as artists she and her partner had very different approaches to their creativity. She'd never realized until going through old entries that a large part of her creative block came from her boyfriend's nine-to-five approach to His art. She had unwittingly put her muse on a schedule to keep His home life balanced. The Warning Signs were there. She just hadn't noticed them as she subconsciously scribbled her thoughts on the page.

Josie, a self-appointed bittergirl, couldn't believe it when she got dumped by her latest guy. "I thought this was the one, I thought we'd have babies, I thought I was going to grow old with Him." Unfortunately, Josie has thought this about her last five boyfriends. Smart, successful, and gorgeous, she's so ready to share her fabulous life with someone that she's composing marriage announcements and mentally combining their furniture before the first date has reached dessert. She rushes into each relationship with such fervor that it's no surprise she knocks over the new guy with all the unattended baggage from her last few fellas. The bittergirls recommend that Josie take a close look at her own Warning Signs before she puts any more "Fragile" labels on herself.

Remember, girls, it's not about blame. Identifying the Warning Signs is simply a way to see them quicker the next time. And as you move from Relationship Mythology to Warning Signs, doesn't it feel great to recognize that He had at least a couple of faults? Good! You're moving in leaps and bounds through your BBRP. You're putting the relationship in the past and in perspective. Admit it, it's hard to cry over a guy who wears white tube socks with black dress shoes, or who tattoos the lyrics to His songs on His arms. While He moans to His next girlfriend about the crumbs she left on the seat of His Audi, you can gloat as you continue on your fabulous bittergirl voyage away from Him.

🍸 bitteractivities

1. Signs, Signs, Everywhere There's Signs   Make a list of all the Warning Signs you've seen and ignored. It can be from this past relationship or several of your relationships combined. Do you see any patterns? Keep your list for one of your **bittergirl bonding nights**. We suspect it will come in handy for at least one of our suggested activities in Chapter 14.

2. He's a Card   Take your favorite, most ridiculous Warning Sign and create a drawing or a quote about it. Make it into a card. Frame it or make copies and send them to friends. Make as many cards as you have Warning Signs. Swap them with your bestbittergirlfriends, use them as wacky affirmations, note cards, or grocery lists. Trust us, they're way more fun than those damn angel cards that give no relationship advice whatsoever.

eight

bittermoms

AH, OUR DEAR, DARLING BITTERMOM. We know you're out there. The bittergirls have watched many a bittermom traipse through the BBRP, attack Relationship Mythology with fervor, laugh off a Warning Sign or four, and then stop suddenly in her tracks and scream, "But I want to kill the fucker! How could He leave me, us, our family?" Beloved bittermom, we hear your cries and we're here to rally around you.

You and He fell in love. You decided to bite the bullet and get married. The wedding bells chimed in glee. But marriage often involves more than just your own two selves in a relationship. Often in your rush to happily ever after, you procreate and produce the nuclear family.

Nuclear Fallout

You just didn't know that with this happily ever after, *nuclear* meant a postapocalyptic explosion that would leave you reeling with a mortgage in one hand and a child in the other, struggling valiantly across the scorched earth on your unpedicured feet.

Some of us want to drive nails through His forehead. Some get depressed. Some blame ourselves—hell, some want to blame and blame and blame someone, anyone, for what has happened. Because it's not right. You didn't sign up for this. It wasn't what you envisioned when you took those vows, unpacked those moving boxes, lay in the maternity ward with your beautiful child in your arms. You wanted to be a family, not a movie of the week starring a has-been television star from the '80s! You wanted a life, a life filled with love and support, and most of all a future. And now thanks to your former Prince Charming you don't have that.

Suddenly you're on your own, licking your wounds, and those salty little suckers are feeling pretty substantial right about now. So how do you get big and strong, manage the household, juggle all the emotional needs of your family, try not to blacken your ex's teeth in all the family portraits while the kids are at school, and not lose your mind? Honey, that's what the bittergirls are here to address.

Child's Play

How to be a bittergirl without raising bitter kids? Well, adjust your halo, straighten your Girl Scout tie, and listen up. No matter why He left, and no matter how crippling His departure has been for you, this is the moment when you need to be the steadiest and most steadfast of rocks for your children. Particularly on the days you most want to hurl a giant boulder at your ex's head! Ironically, when all around you is crumbling, when you feel as if the very ground you stand on is falling away from you like the floor of a carnival funhouse, *you must suck it up and be a grown-up* no matter how precarious the funhouse may be. Now more than ever your kids need you to be not just functional but thinking, honest, responsible, and well behaved.

However difficult, the only way through this quagmire of guilt, hatred, and recrimination is to rise above it and deal with your new-found situation with decorum.

It's not the kids' fault that all this happened, and for their sakes, it's got to be nobody's fault. Doesn't matter what happened with the grown-ups; this is the moment you have to be more than you ever thought you could be and take one on the chin for the family.

What happened between the two of you was between the two of you. The kids aren't your best friends or confidantes. They're just your kids. It's times like this when you need your fellow bittergirls to let it all hang out with, to get wild with, to talk about your elaborate plans for revenge with. (The operative word here is *talk*. . . .)

You need to gather your bestbittergirlfriends around you and lean on them. If you have to complain, complain to them. When you want to wail at three o'clock in the morning, phone one of them. If you need to go out and get stupid, book a babysitter and go out on the town with your bestbittergirlfriends. Because that's what they're here for.

Your kids, on the other hand, are not. Your kids still love their dad, and so they should. Now, physical and mental abuse are another matter entirely, and if that's what's going on in your home, then baby, the rules are different and you shouldn't be reading this book, you should be filing charges. But if you're not physically but psychically bruised, reeling from the unexpectedness of His departure or His idiocy, don't share this information with the kids.

Let your crazies out with your team, and do the adolescent stuff you have to do, *need* to do for your own sanity, then come home and tuck your kids in and tell them that everything is going to be all right. Because it will. Because you love them, and you're going to make damn sure that everything in their world is as right as you can make it.

They're your kids and they deserve to have a childhood. So repeat after us: "I am the grown-up, they are the children."

Blame on You

As if dealing with your own free fall of emotions isn't enough, you have to remember that myriad feelings will be running through your child's mind at this point, just as they are yours. If you're having difficulty coming to terms with the end of your relationship, imagine how difficult it is for your child to make sense of it. You have to remember that feelings are facts—you cannot negate anything your child is feeling. You have to deal with it. And how a three-year-old deals with the disintegration of Mommy and Daddy's relationship is very different from how a thirteen-year-old will. Your explanation has to be age-appropriate and in terms your child will understand. In all the confusion and rearranging of households, you may end up getting the blame for turning their world upside down. Sure it's not fair, but who said anything about fair in those Lamaze classes? Someday they'll understand, but right now they may need you to be the emotional punching bag.

The Bittergirl Institute for Advanced Research on Dumping has compiled a list of "Cuts Like a Knife" comments and questions that continue to pierce bittermoms' hearts worldwide, and how a grownup bittermom can best handle them:

The kids say: "Why did Daddy leave?"

What you want to say: "Because Daddy is a thirty-eight-going-on-ten-year-old dickhead who never made me come in all the years we were together."

What grown-up you actually says: "Although Mommy and Daddy don't love each other anymore, our love for you will never end. Sometimes adults need to be alone, and sometimes even though daddies love their children very much, they can't live with their families. But above all, whatever is happening between Mommy and Daddy has nothing to do with how much we love you because that is a different kind of love and it is a love that never wavers."

The kids say: "I want to go and live with Daddy."
What you want to say: "Daddy and His twenty-one-year-old knocked-up secretary don't have the room in their apartment over her parents' garage."
What grown-up you actually says: "Well, you see, Daddy and I spent a long time talking about this, and He and I decided that it would be better for you to live with me in our old house. But more than anything else in the whole wide world, Daddy loves you. And the hardest thing that Daddy has ever done in His life was leaving our house where we all lived together. Because there is nothing in Daddy's life that He likes better than waking up in the room down the hall from you."

The kids say: "Why didn't Daddy come and pick me up like He said he would?"
What you want to say: "Because Daddy is a lard-ass with the attention span of a gnat and can't commit to a job or a relationship let alone a play date at McDonald's."
What grown-up you actually says: "Daddy called to say how sorry He was that He didn't get to see you today but He was very busy finding food and shelter for a boatload of refugees and tending to their wounds by tearing the fabric from His very own clothes! He'll call you after He's finished landing a helicopter full of starving children on the rooftop of a multimillionaire with philanthropic interests. Your Daddy is so brave."

The kids say: "It's all your fault that Daddy left."
What you want to say: "That's right. Daddy left because He didn't like having someone cook and clean for Him, raise His

kids, share the financial responsibilities, remember His mother's birthday, let Him win at Monopoly Junior, and screw me blind with His black dress socks still on!"

What grown-up you actually says: "You know what? When Daddy first told me that He couldn't live here anymore, I got mad because I wanted Him to stay living with us. It's a crummy thing for grown-ups to do to kids, change their world around, but it doesn't mean you don't have a Daddy, and it doesn't mean that your Daddy loves you any less; it just means you don't get quite as much of Him as you used to before. But that's okay—you can get mad at me about that. You're allowed. Someday you'll see that it's nobody's fault."

Now, however much you want to tell the kids that Daddy's new friend's boobs cost twenty thousand bucks and that her hair isn't really blonde or that Daddy doesn't live with you anymore because He's a spineless asshole who wanted a new sports car more than a family, don't do it! A bittergirl knows that the barest of facts are all that children need to know. So tell them what they need to hear. Then after they're tucked up in bed for the night or out with Daddy for a spin in His shiny new car, you can stick your head in the freezer and let out the mother of all screams because, honey, you are on the fast track to martyrdom.

After her ex walked out on her and the kids, Jean took to playing a little game with herself. Every time she said "Your father" to her kids she said "The Fucker" in her head.

The Spy Who Loves Me

So it's Sunday night and the kids have just returned from a weekend at Daddy's. You sit them on the hardest chair you own and shine the interrogation light in their eyes. "What did you do at Daddy's? Stuff? What kind of stuff? Where did you go? Did you eat? What did you eat? Well how many green vegetables were on your plate? Did He paint His kitchen yet? What shade of yellow? 'I don't know' isn't a shade. Who was there? Was she there? Did He mention me? What did He say about me? Did you remind Him about the check? It was your duty to your country to come home with a check! You forgot your boots? Great. Now our whole operation is blown. Our cover is ruined because you forgot your boots."

Oh bittermom, whatever you do, do not send your kids to Daddy's as though they're leaving MI5 on a top-secret mission. If you want information that desperately, spring for a private investigator to keep you apprised of how many of the recommended food groups your ex is feeding the kids. Do not use them as carrier pigeons, emissaries, or moles. Let your lawyer do your dirty work and let them be kids hanging out with their dad. Then when they want to join the CIA, at least they'll be getting paid for it.

Petra and Rachel walk their kids to school every morning. In the year following her breakup Petra would bitch about her ex Callum and vent her frustrations. When Petra discovered that Rachel and Callum were seeing each other she flew into a rage and actually pulled her kids out of the school that Rachel's kids attended.

👄 bittergirlspeak

Petra, Petra, Petra. Shame on you! Keep the schoolyard fights in the schoolyard. While Rachel's behavior is Anti-Bittergirl, punishing your children is NEVER excusable. They've had enough to deal with watching their parents' marriage dissolve, and taking them away from all their friends because you're mad at yours is absolute non-bittergirl behavior.

Moving On Up

Numerous bittergirls have told us of rising above and moving on, meanwhile worrying what all this is doing to their children. What will they learn about male–female relationships? You can't worry about that. You can have friends and relatives with good strong bonds, relationships where two equal partners treat each other with dignity and respect, and you can let your kids know in no uncertain terms that that's the way men and women are supposed to treat each other. There will always be examples in your world that you can show your children. In addition, you can demonstrate to your kids that even though Mommy and Daddy split up, they can still behave like normal civilized human beings.

In reality, there may be yelling, and there may be frustration and angst and hair-pulling and catcalling too. But here's the point: *not in front of the kids.* They should not be privy to emotions and arguments and concepts they're not yet mentally prepared for. That's not to say you're not going to be honest with them; but you can only be as honest as they are old enough to deal with. Don't sugarcoat things, don't give them false hope that Daddy and Mommy are going to work it out and live happily ever after, but lay it out as best you can. Even if you lie in bed wrapped up in Relationship Mythology, don't share it with your kids.

It can all be difficult to cope with and will take some thought, preparation, and hard work, but the idea of this being a permanent situation should come from both partners. Remember: You've come this far in your BBRP, and you can keep going.

Bittergirls know who the grown-ups are. And they don't forget it.

The High Road

Lots of bittergirls have found themselves feeling like the bad cop in the newly redefined family. If Mom is the custodial parent, then often Mom has a career, helps with the homework, runs the errands, goes to the parent–teacher conferences, bakes the muffins for the bake sale, doesn't manage to get her roots done, and shows up at the PTA meeting wearing her slippers and an inside-out T-shirt. Dad gets to swoop in on the weekend and be the "fun guy." Who wouldn't resent that?

Sure, spoiling the kids might seem like the easiest way to earn their love—in the short term. But who wants a kid no one can stand? The bittergirls love a polite, articulate child—but we can all spot a mile away the kid who's learned to play his or her divorced parents off each other. Teach your kids to be healthy and strong and self-reliant by example. The way you were raising them before The Incident is the way you should raise them afterward—they want that consistency and only you can give it to them.

Stuart left Jill when baby Leigh was three months old. Jill raised her daughter without uttering a single bitter word about Him. When, as an adult, Leigh decided she wanted to find her father, Jill encouraged her and wished her luck. Leigh connected with Stuart and all He did was bad-mouth her mother. Leigh cut off all contact. When she came home, she told Jill she was the best mother ever and thanked her for giving her a childhood where she didn't have to be an adult.

💋 bittergirlspeak

Ah, Jill. Now that is the bittergirl behavior we love to see.

We're not saying that you should be a patsy or shoulder the burden of the breakup. We are saying, don't expect your kids to go on this journey with you. They need to be Switzerland, and the only way they can do that is if you allow them their neutrality. Follow the BBRP and let go of the guilt that everything and anything your kids are feeling right now is your fault. In the midst of your heartache you may not feel like the perfect mother—but who is? You are the perfect mother for your children—simply because you're their mother. They don't need June Cleaver, they just need you.

Sure it might not be the family you envisioned when you first started out on the path to domestic bliss, but you owe it to yourself and your kids to make it the best you possibly can. He's their dad and like it or not He's the only one they have. And you're their mom and you're the only one they have. It's your family's life; let's see what you can make of it.

Because love and loyalty and commitment to family are also part of the bittergirl way.

🍸 bitteractivities

1. Subcontract for Bittermoms   To be read and signed by all newly single bittermoms.

I WILL NOT UNDER ANY CIRCUMSTANCES use the children as an excuse to see Him.

I WILL NOT UNDER ANY CIRCUMSTANCES pump my children for information on how He's doing.

I WILL NOT UNDER ANY CIRCUMSTANCES let Him get away with anything less than what He should be doing for the children.

I WILL FAITHFULLY PROMISE to keep my children's best interests at heart at all times.

I WILL FAITHFULLY PROMISE to ask Him for what is fair throughout, monetarily and physically, because I will not short-change my children through any misguided sense of martyrdom.

I WILL FAITHFULLY PROMISE to remember at all times that my children are intelligent, thinking human beings who will grow up and draw their own conclusions about what happened to their parents.

I WILL FAITHFULLY PROMISE to not try to be all things to all people, but to be the best parent I can be under the circumstances and with what is available to me.

I WILL FAITHFULLY PROMISE to tell them I love them every day and show them by caring for them first and foremost.

I WILL FAITHFULLY PROMISE to look after myself because my children need me, and I need me too.

2. Go to Chapter 11: "Bittersweet Revenge"   Take your basest instincts out on those exercises, not on the psyches of your kids.

3. Count the Trash   Count up the number of times a day you slip up and trash your ex to your children. *Make a game out of it for yourself,* and over a week's time see if you can get the number down to—we don't know, possibly . . . none?

4. Our Family Now   Put up a bulletin board or section off part of the kitchen wall or fridge and save the pictures, notes, photos, and mementos that speak to you of the love in your newly reconfigured family. *Make it into a shrine, a collage of love* to see you through the bad times. Make sure it's in a place where you'll see it often.

nine

the anti-bittergirl

YOU'VE MET HER. You know her. Oh yes, there will come a time when every fledgling bittergirl is just getting her feet back on the ground, her stilettos solidly on her two nicely pedicured feet, when she runs up against that brick wall called the Anti-Bittergirl. For every fabulous friend you have, for all the support and the wondrous gift those women and men have given you, there always has to be a fly in the ointment, a shark in the sea.

You can be anywhere. At a dinner party you'll hear that your good friend Tasha—who was just telling you the other night, as she dug for the dirt on the whole breakup, that He was a bastard and should pay for His evil ways—well apparently Tasha had Him and His new squeeze over for dinner the very next evening. Over drinks with your friends Martha pulls you aside and tells you that the kicky new blouse you treated yourself to doesn't look so good on you—yellow really makes you look kind of sallow. Francesca laughs when she runs into you on the street and says, "Wow, most people *lose* weight when they break up with someone." It can even happen in the privacy of your own home: His overly sweet little junior assistant phones you to ask for His parents' phone number because she has to RSVP for two to a family dinner and she just didn't know who else to ask, now that He's on that scuba trip to the Bahamas and she can't reach Him. Or maybe it's when your child asks you why your former confidante Margie was sitting on Daddy's lap at dinner at His place last night?

These are the friends no bittergirl needs. There is solidarity in the world, and these people aren't providing it. It's time to prune the friendship tree and KICK HER OUT OF THE CLUB.

And a good thing too. One of the things that a Brutal Breakup can provide is a clear map of who a bittergirl's real friends are. Their acts of kindness and sympathy and patience and goodness make a sad contrast with the kind of treatment we wouldn't mete out to our least favorite goldfish.

famous anti-bittergirls

Liz Taylor

Marla Maples

Camilla Parker-Bowles

Winona Ryder

Angelina Jolie

Monica Lewinsky

Trisha Yearwood

Scarlett O'Hara

Claire Danes

Sure, every bittergirl has indulged in naughty conduct. In fact, in her BBRP every bittergirl needs to go out on the town and indulge in some pretty adolescent behavior. Twenty years' worth of data collected by The Bittergirl Institute for Advanced Research on Dumping prove beyond a doubt that such behavior at this stage in the BBRP is vital and absolutely essential for total mental health. Bad bittergirl forms of behavior include staying out until 4 A.M. and waking up in front of the toilet with the seat line marked semipermanently across your forehead, putting pins through the eyes of your formerly favorite picture of Him, even following Him at a discreet distance as He goes about His Saturday morning errands, and planning the violence you want to inflict on Him. All these activities, so long as they don't get out of hand, are not only expected but necessary, and in fact recommended as part of the crucial BBRP timetable.

But the Anti-Bittergirl is different. There are rules of engagement in life and in love and in breakups, and no bittergirl would ever hurt another intentionally. Not so the Anti-Bittergirl. The Anti-Bittergirl lives to take advantage of your weakest moments. She's watching your guy before the dumping even goes down. The Anti-Bittergirl has her eye on the main chance, and if you're providing an opportunity in your time of distress, all the better: It just paves her way.

Our adolescent behavior in the BBRP usually takes fairly harmless forms, although a year from now we may blush to remember that we spent so much time and energy on these activities. But they can't be helped: Crooning "I Honestly Love You" fifteen times a day into His answering machine; bursting into tears at the sight of His favorite brand of nacho chips in your local variety store . . . for more advice on these moments, turn in your handbook to Chapter 12 and study up on Bittergirl Breakdowns. We as bittergirls are here to listen and nod patiently until we know that the time has come for you to turn the page and move on.

But the Anti-Bittergirls will take advantage. They will listen to your tale of woe, hold your hand and nod, and then just when you're at your weakest they'll turn on you. They'll use your fragility in the workplace to suggest you're not up to handling that fabulous new position you created in your extensive cost-cutting breakdown of office procedures. She is also the girl who aided in the breakup, whether by cutting you down, taking over your man, telling you that you should dump Him and then moving in on Him herself, or sleeping with Him before or immediately after your relationship with Him was over.

These are the Anti-Bittergirls, and the bittergirls are here to tell you to Kick Them Out of the Club. They don't belong here.

A Field Guide to the Subspecies of Anti-Bittergirl

Crazy Girl

Crazy Girl. You had a feeling, an instinct. You knew something was wrong. So you girded your loins and confronted Crazy Girl with your fears about her behavior with your guy, only to be told "Dag? And me? You must be crazy!" Dag heard about it and told you that you were crazy too, and for a solid year you believed them and doubted yourself and even took yourself to a shrink to deal with your obsessive and "crazy" behavior. Then Crazy Girl's eminently sane brother hunted you down at the gym and told you he couldn't live with himself any longer without telling you that Dag was sleeping with his sister.

The only crazy thing you did was ignore your instincts, sugar. Now, you go crazy and tell her she doesn't belong here: She's no bittergirl, baby.

Office Bitch

She flirted with Him over the copier and draped herself all over Him on the dance floor at the office Christmas party while you were stuck talking to Herb the Pocket Protector King from accounting. No cliché was too clichéd for our Office Bitch, who made it very clear to everyone else on their corporate team that she was out to get Him, and He fell for it. What's a bittergirl to do? KICK HER OUT OF THE CLUB.

Ladder Climber

"Oh, Ms. Jones," she'll breathe heavily into your fabulous, trusting supervisor's ear over double espressos at break time, "I'm a little worried about Bethany's stability right now. You know what a big fan I am of her work and how fantastic I think she is, but she's under a lot of strain right now in her" (voice dropping to a whisper as she wrinkles her nose distastefully to show how pained she is to have to bring up such a delicate subject) "Personal Life—it might not be the best time for her right now. . . ." At this point her voice trails to almost nothing but then picks up as she brightly suggests: "Just let me know if there's anything I can do to help. HR has always been a keen interest of mine here at Acme Corp. . . ." And with a twist of the knife the deed is done. Sorry, but no bittergirl will use another's pain to hike up the corporate ladder. She is so out of here.

If you catch her in time you may actually have to thank the Ladder Climber for bringing you back to reality with a much-needed shock to the system. Love is love and getting dumped is painful, but losing your job over Him? Not the bittergirl way.

Potty Mouth

She was one of the gang. She was a staple at every dinner party. She always seemed so interested in everybody's lives. She'd remember to phone you on your birthday or ask Him how things were going with that difficult client.

But as soon as she hears the news about your breakup she spews expletives about Him that would rival the Exorcist. She bad-mouths everything He represented. She "never wanted to say anything but" . . . she always hated Him, she had a feeling. She knew He was bad news. She didn't think you could handle the truth so she put on a happy face about it all.

Hello, Potty Mouth. Potty Mouth is a know-it-all but she's never gone out on a limb herself. It's far safer for her to comment on other people's lives because she doesn't have a life of her own. Your misery makes her feel superior. It confirms her choice to do nothing but be a bystander in life. You need friends that live smack dab in the middle of life, warts and all. So wash her mouth out with soap, stuff a sock in it, and send her on her way.

After The Incident, the last thing Sophia wanted to do was defend her ex to anybody. So when her perpetually single friend Hilary heard about her breakup and exclaimed in front of a roomful of people, "Well, it's no surprise, I was just waiting for Him to come out of the closet!" it took all of Sophia's strength to quietly defend Nathan and His sexuality.

Drama Queen

There's always something going on with Sandy. She's always helping people—dropping off a casserole after Andrea's appendectomy, sitting shiva when Zayde Goldblum died, rearranging the food display at Louise's bridal shower just to get it out of the sun. Her emotions run high. They hover close to the surface. She'll laugh with you, she'll cry with you. She'll arrive by your side the moment disaster hits.

So when He dumps you, Sandy is the first one ringing your doorbell, with a box of tissues in one hand and a platter of egg salad sandwiches in the other (which she's taking to her sister-in-law's cousin's wake). She urges you to share your grief. She wants to be there for you. She weeps with you as you relay your story. It seems compassionate and kind until three months later when she's still crying over your breakup. "You guys were the ideal couple. This is devastating. What hope is there for me?" And you end up consoling her.

Ah, the Drama Queen. Also known as a professional mourner, the Drama Queen cashes in on everyone else's occasions, happy or sad. It's all about her. It's all drama, all the time. She takes your breakup and makes it her own in her insatiable quest for attention. Ditch the Drama Queen. Her world revolves around herself so much, she likely won't even notice. She'll be busy riding the wave of someone else's tragedy and throwing herself on Zayde Goldblum's coffin along with her shovelful of dirt.

Maddy was touched that her friend Shelly was so concerned for her well-being in the aftermath of her breakup. While they'd always been close, Maddy was surprised by Shelly's daily visits to drop off food and her phone calls "just to check in." But as Maddy navigated her way through her BBRP, she felt she was moving on from her breakup faster than Shelly was. Shelly still wept when she heard Maddy and Tom's song, and no matter what they talked about Shelly always managed to bring the conversation back to the breakup and how much it had devastated her hopes of happily ever after. Maddy eventually took to screening Shelly's calls until a mutual friend informed her that Shelly's boss's sister had not only been dumped but right at the altar. Faster than Maddy could say "Shelly to the rescue!" there she was helping the caterers pack away the food and freeze-drying the bouquets.

Two-Faced Wonder

Denise. Denise was your best friend. A best friend through and through. The best friend who told you all her secrets. The best friend who laughed with you and spent dateless Saturday nights with you and a bottle of Beaujolais. The best friend who squealed with delight when gorgeous fireman Dan appeared in your life. The best friend who frowned as He began to call more and more often. The best friend who would laugh with you at the funny things He said and then when He turned away pull a face and mimic Him. The best friend who slowly planted the seeds of discontent in your ear, who told you over and over again that He just wasn't good enough for you. The best friend who held your hand when the inevitable breakup occurred and reassured you that it was all for the best. The best friend who then suddenly disappeared from your life. Until six months later you received Dan and Denise's wedding invitation.

Good old Denise. We have scrubbed her name off the gilded list of Bittergirl Alumnae.

Or after The Incident she drove you home, she held your hand, she told you you were so strong. Then dropped you off and hightailed it to your ex's for a little of that loving she'd gotten used to during the last two months of your relationship, two months before He even got around to telling you that it was over.

We don't even need to dignify this Anti-Bittergirl by revoking her bittergirl membership: She was never close to being one of us.

The Stealth Bomber

It's subtle; it's small. But it hurts nonetheless. Her timing is impeccable: She'll pick the moment when you're at your worst. She hates to tell you this but . . . and she'll dump a load of emotional napalm right in your lap. Or better yet, she'll choose the moment when you're starting to come to and face the world again. When you make your first solo outing after the breakup, the Stealth Bomber will come round a corner and with a delicate wrinkle of her nose ask why you chose that particular dress to wear tonight—

oh no reason, it's just, well, your hips . . . and she'll shrug, laugh, and run off, leaving carnage in her wake.

Giselle was surprised to learn that a bunch of her friends had been invited to their pal Mary's cottage. This was a group that regularly went away together. Giselle thought Mary had simply forgotten to call her or had assumed she already knew until Giselle phoned her to find out what was going on. Mary paused for a moment and said, "Look, I'm sorry Giselle, honey, but it's a couples thing. You understand, don't you?" Before Giselle had time to respond, Mary trilled, "Knew you would! All righty, have a great weekend!"

The Stealth lives for your misery; she takes great pleasure in carpet-bombing. Your only recompense is that she'll never understand the pleasure of other bittergirls' company, because of course she'll never gain membership in the great worldwide sorority.

How to Spot an Anti-Bittergirl
Before She's Done Damage

Sometimes it's actually easy to spot an Anti-Bittergirl. She's the woman who has no other female friends. She'll say it's because she finds men so much easier to get along with, or that she "just doesn't have anything in common with other women." Nothing in common? What about breasts, menstrual cycles, the weather, Johnny Depp? The Anti-Bittergirl has a new best friend every week. This week it's someone who's going through a rough time in her marriage, but she'll be replaced next week by someone else who just discovered that her decorator is color-blind. She'll take you to the bar to drown your sorrows with tequila shooters, but she'll leave you puking in the bathroom while she salsas into a cab with the cute busboy. The Anti-Bittergirl doesn't hesitate to tell you when your ex is seeing somebody new, or that He doesn't seem to be grieving the relationship at all. She'll still expect you to go bridesmaid-dress shopping a week after The Incident and she'll see no problem in regaling you with her lover's sexual assets. She views your breakup as a project or its particulars as a password to this week's dinner party. The more details you provide her with, the more ammunition you supply to validate her own choices.

When a friend's interest in your relationship is just a little too curious for your liking, trust your instinct. We all want our friends to be happy, but we're usually too caught up in our own lives to show THAT much concern. If she smells like an Anti-Bittergirl and looks like an Anti-Bittergirl, she's an Anti-Bittergirl.

Steps to Dump an Anti-Bittergirl

With this kind of manipulative individual, honesty may not always be the best policy. Remember that this is someone who turns other people's traumas into her own, so just imagine the production that dumping a bitterbitch could elicit. Should you dump her, be prepared to find yourself the bad guy in her telling of the tale. If you're up for it, then keep it simple.

> "I appreciate your interest in what I'm going through right now, but I think I need to deal with this on my own for the time being."
>
> *or*
>
> "I appreciate your interest in what I'm going through right now, but I've just discovered that you've been fucking both my ex and my shrink and therefore I don't feel comfortable confiding in you anymore."

If you aren't at the point in your BBRP where you can shoulder yet another emotional confrontation, then a little white lie to spare you the wrath of the Anti-Bittergirl may make your life a tad easier.

"I appreciate your interest in what I'm going through right now, but I just got a call from my cousin in the Yukon and she's invited me to go mining for gold to get my mind off things. I'll be in touch."

or

"I appreciate your interest in what I'm going through right now, but my new Spanish lover, Ramone, didn't I mention him? He feels a little shy about my friends knowing all about our sex life, I told you about his abs, right? I didn't? Well anyway I'm going to have to be a little more discreet about what's going on with me. Isn't it funny, the things he can do with his tongue—yet he's so bashful!"

What to Do If Anti-Bittergirl Turns into SuperBitch Anti-Bittergirl (and Won't Go Away)

Call the police.

When you're healed, when you're whole, you can look back at these poor twisted souls and shake your head in wonder. How have they gotten this far in life without knowing the joys that come from the sisterhood? Like characters in a fairy tale, they'll never see the world in all its glorious beauty because they've got their heads down plotting the destruction of others' happiness. Too bad—they're not bittergirls. They probably never will be. Their loss. Members only. And we know who we are.

🍸 bitteractivities

1. List of Shame   List the Anti-Bittergirls you know. What's their Anti-Bittergirl trait and why are they in your life? Make a plan to dump them, and do it.

2. Buffer Zone   Even if you kick the Anti-Bittergirls out of your life, you may still have to deal with them: at work, at the gym, at family gatherings. Enlist your team to help you develop your line from Chapter 3 so that you have the perfect auto-reply to shut them down and keep the breathing space around you pure. Make sure the team knows exactly who the Anti-Bittergirls are so they can implement the game strategies from Chapter 3.

3. Anti-Bittergirl Pie   Make a pie chart. Make it into a pie. Or any delightful treat you love. Invite your BBGFs over and make like when you were a kid: Remember when you didn't want to eat your supper and Mommy made you eat the kids you didn't like in your class? (Here comes Gavin!) Divvy up the pie and revel in chomping down on all those nasty anti-forces that used to invade your life. If you're going to make it symbolic it might as well be something you can savor.

ten

the plot thickens

AH, BITTERGIRL. Our beloved bittergirl. Isn't it amazing? Here you are actually having moments where you're thinking about things other than Him. The minutes don't always feel like hours, and the hours don't always feel like days. The word *recovery* in the Bittergirl Breakup Recovery Period is starting to have real meaning. In fact, months might have passed since The Incident, and you're still breathing and walking, aren't you? Some days you even manage to look in the mirror and feel attractive. See, you didn't die. He didn't break you. You've probably completely rediscovered yourself. You finally cut off the long hair He always loved and are looking wildly sexy with a messy bob in that burnt auburn color. For the first time in your life you've maximized your gym membership. The box-aerobics instructor has even approached you to suggest you train to teach the class one day. Bjorn, your massage therapist, says seeing you every Monday is the highlight of his week. And who knew there are more shades of nail polish in your tones than you could try in a year?

You've been able to change the message on your answering machine yourself! When people ask you about Him you can look them in the eye without shame and say, "We're not together anymore." You no longer cry at the first-time home-buyer commercials. You haven't ordered anything from an infomercial in months. When you see flowers you stop to smell them instead of thinking, "What's the point? They'll just wilt and die eventually." People are telling you how incredible you look, that you're positively glowing. You're starting to believe them. You're buoyed up on this new interest being shown in you, the new glances and stares from strangers. You may even be starting to think you're getting your Kernel back.

Congratulations, BUT beware.

Yes, you've cut your hair. Yes, you've dyed it. You've shed fifteen pounds. Your pride is starting to take shape again. You've been manicured, pedicured, massaged, and you're out on Tuesday nights sharing martinis with the girls. You're occasionally startled by the sound of your own laugh. You're beginning to feel that somewhere inside you the person you loved in yourself is emerging again. And this is the prime time for the devilish clutch of temptation to grab you. Admit it. You're plotting to get Him back. Whether it's the minuscule thought of bumping into Him in a hot new skintight dress or the full-on staging of a life-threatening operation, you're enticed by the prospect of luring Him back into your life.

Remember, the bittergirls are not about judgment. We've been there. We know these feelings. They're inevitable. Your self-worth is often so tied up in Him that once you have it back you think He might just change His mind about you.

The point is, it's you who's changed. You've grown. Remember all those clichés of mourning the relationship, dealing with it? Well, you've done that. And you don't carve all that misery out of yourself without becoming slightly different, slightly wiser. Maybe you're a little more cynical, maybe your sense of humor has a little more bite and a little less magic, maybe you're harder, or maybe you're just more realistic. Whatever it is, this journey you've been on is one *you've* traveled. You're the one who's been trekking through the BBRP. And what about Him? Do you think He's changed? Do you think He's done the same kind of soul-searching, asked Himself all the maybe-ifs or the what-would-I-have-done-differentlys?

The day Franca and Jamie broke up she gathered her three best-bittergirlfriends together for an evening of soul-searching, tears, and support over the kitchen table and several bottles of red wine. Jamie headed out for an evening with the boys. When He turned up the next day to pick up His stuff Franca asked Him what the boys had talked about, knowing the intimacy and support she had shared with the girls the previous evening. Jamie shrugged and said, "We had a beer, watched the game, and then went out and hit a bucket of balls. It was good." So no, odds are He has not been out exploring His inner soul.

There are so many reasons we plot to get Him back. The bittergirls have said and heard them all. No one will ever understand me like He did. No one's family could ever be as welcoming and wonderful. No one else will find my G-spot. No one else could possibly think the bump on my nose is "cute." No one else will want to spend New Year's playing Scrabble and drinking guava juice. No one else will sprinkle our bed with rose petals on our anniversary. No one else will have my favorite Swiss chocolate bar delivered the day before my period each month. No one else will want to read my public school storybooks. No one else will appreciate my vinyl collection.

Honey, there are always going to be things He was great at in your relationship, but need we remind you of the dangers of Relationship Mythology? You absolutely can't get stuck playing them over and over again in your mind.

As you journey farther through the BBRP sometimes you're fully aware that you're plotting to get Him back. But sometimes it's just a subconscious desire that manifests itself in subtle or not-so-subtle behaviors. After consulting data gathered by The Bittergirl Institute for Advanced Research on Dumping, we've profiled some of the typical Plot Traps that bittergirls fall into. Even if you're aware that you're plotting to get Him back, you might not realize how far you're actually willing to go.

Plot Traps

Hotshot

You're obsessed with your appearance. Your nails are immaculate thanks to your weekly manicure and pedicure. Your hair is perfectly styled and colored (don't those highlights look spectacular!). You've discovered the joy of facials and invested in a new line of makeup (it all matches now!). You're working out, lifting weights, counting the reps to His name—Charlie 1, Charlie 2, Charlie 3, Charlie 4. Between the gym, your marathon training, and your twice-weekly yoga classes you've lost inches and your figure is slim and strong, with exquisitely sculpted muscles. You took yourself shopping and splurged on a fantastic new wardrobe to fit your sleek new body. You look in the mirror and think, I look fabulous. How could He not want me back?

💋 bittergirlspeak

Hmm, if He loves you just for your looks, honey, you're in big trouble. What happens when you're eighty and drooling? Or are you going to spend your life savings getting the latest surgeries and services just so you can look good for Him? We think it's fantastic that you look good. So look good for you!

Janine had always thought she needed to lose some weight. So after Damien left her she shed some pounds, went out and bought a new wardrobe, and changed her hair too. She was looking pretty fantastic when Damien called and said He wanted to meet her "to talk." She turned a few heads as she walked to the table—for three? Damien was sitting there with a woman who could have been a carbon copy of the old Janine: pleasant, a little overweight, dressed in standard office issue with Janine's old style of hair. Damien introduced her as His fiancée Diane. He said He just didn't feel right about letting Janine read about the engagement in the paper, and that's why they'd wanted to meet with her.

After Janine made peace with the fact that she'd lost the weight with an eye to getting Damien back, she calmed down a bit. She kept the wardrobe and the hair, and learned to appreciate her slimmed-down body for herself. Today she says that if she hadn't gotten dumped, she would have stayed in the same old clothes and the same old body. She's happy with how she looks now—for herself.

Daydreamer

You haven't left the house, you haven't washed your hair in weeks or gotten out of your pajamas, but you spend your days daydreaming of the night you bump into Him at His favorite bar. He tells you how stunning you look. He's made the biggest mistake of His life and He wants you back. He orders a bottle of Veuve Clicquot and tells the bartender that you've got something big to celebrate—the rest of your lives together. Everyone at the bar bursts into applause because He's spent the last thirty-two Thursday nights crying into His beer over you. The waitress comes over and gives you a hug. She says she feels like she knows you because all He's been able to talk about is you, your smile, your beauty, your thoughtfulness, your generosity, your way with people. He interrupts her by grabbing your hand and holding out a stunning platinum ring with a diamond rock. Will you marry me?

👄 bittergirlspeak

Honey, if you haven't been out of the house or washed your hair or peeled off your pajamas, odds are you're not going to wow Him when you walk into that bar. He may just plug His nose and cry into His beer for an entirely different reason. Here's a daydream for you to focus on. You take off your clothes, step into the shower, blow-dry your hair, put on some makeup, and go for a walk in the fresh air. We guarantee that's a daydream to build the rest of your life on. And Veuve Clicquot? How much do you want to bet He thinks that's somewhere near your G-spot?

Coincidence? I Think Not

On your way home from work you wander the aisles of His local grocery store feigning interest in the seasonal organic produce. You befriend one of the part-time clerks and offer him twenty bucks to page you if your ex comes into the store when you're not there. Or you dress yourself up in your one and only Chanel suit and wander the stacks of His favorite local library, extremely intent on finding an out-of-print book. Or you convince one of your bestbittergirl-friends to exchange cars with you for a week so you can sit outside His house without Him knowing it's you. When you do bump into Him you pretend it's a huge coincidence that you should see Him there. Coincidence? I think not. It must be meant to be.

👄 bittergirlspeak

Repeat to yourself: I am a stalker. I am a stalker. I am a stalker. And if you don't stop stalking Him, you might end up with a restraining order. Why not start dating the grocery store clerk or chat up one of the librarians instead of wasting your time on Him? If you insist on all-night stakeouts, go get your private investigator's license so that at least you'll get paid for it!

Best Friend Barter

You call His best friend just to say hi and to see how he's doing. You tell him you miss hanging out with him. You offer him box tickets to this weekend's NBA game. You've got a great girlfriend you think he'd hit it off with and it would be a good chance for them to meet. And then you suggest he bring your ex too—you know how much He loves the Knicks. Why would He pass up free tickets?

💋 bittergirlspeak

Do you really want His best friend to see how desperate you are? And what if He does pass up the free tickets—how humiliating would that be? Here's an idea. Why don't you offer to wash His best friend's car every weekend until you get Him back. Or you could do His best friend's laundry. If that doesn't take up too much of your time, you could offer to walk b.f.'s dog on your lunch break or drop off a nice packed lunch at b.f.'s place each morning. That way you might get Him back, and it's cheaper than tickets to pro games. Dignity, ladies, use it as a verb.

Work It

You arrange a meeting with His boss to a) talk about the possibility of some contract work; b) offer a free lunch 'n' learn Conflict Resolution session that should be mandatory for His team; c) set up an account with the company and request that He be the executive in charge of handling your business; d) see if you can get invited to the company Christmas party. How can He say no to His boss?

👄 bittergirlspeak

Remember, you have to work again in this town. Do you really want people talking about you as that crazy ex who wouldn't leave Him alone? You know how small the world is. Save face and don't wreck your career as well as your self-esteem. Go and rent *Single White Female*. Look in the mirror.

Kid Card

You call to tell Him that Patrick needs a ride to hockey practice. Some of the girls are coming over for a lingerie party at your place and you can't drive Patty in case you miss the lingerie delivery. When He shows up to get Patty, you just happen to be trying on the merchandise and answer the door in a frilly red lace number. And Patty? Oh, little Finbar down the road just joined the team and his mom kindly offered to drive them. You tried to call but His cell mustn't have had a signal. Does He want to come in and talk about daycare?

👄 bittergirlspeak

Refer to Chapter 8: "Bittermoms." NEVER EVER use the child as an excuse to get His attention. You know what happens when you cry wolf, and little Patty should not have to pay for your behavior.

Stuff Exchange

Every week you manage to find something around your house/apartment/condo that He's left behind and just cannot live without. You unearth one black sock that must be His, and you know how frustrated He gets when there's only one black sock in the sock drawer. You decide He must have it NOW and so show up at His doorstep, sock in hand. You discover His old favorite hockey sweater—the one He wore when His grandfather took Him to the play-offs. It's the middle of summer but that's okay because you know from following Him that He's playing in a summer league on Monday nights with the guys from university. Once He sees the sock or the hockey jersey He'll realize that He left half His emotional life with you too, right?

bittergirlspeak

Doesn't He have stuff of yours? Has He been making an effort to drop it off to you? If He needed that one black sock so desperately, He'd phone to see if you have it. But here's a thought—wouldn't you rather get the satisfaction of burning His stuff or having a yard sale and making some money off Him? You could even advertise it as "Getting rid of the rat's shit."

Sick Alert

You research rare diseases online and at the library. You're reading up on spleenectomies and uncommon chronic illnesses that you can be diagnosed as having. You plan a day operation. You'll gain His support, His love, through this terrible time. When He offers to drive you to the hospital you tell Him that no, it's okay, your bestbittergirlfriends have taken care of things. Your kid is in on it too, and you've got a makeup person booked for the day to help you look wan. You've printed out an agenda of the day's procedure, conveniently placing Him at your bedside when you arrive home—weak and pale and exhausted. How could He not fall back in love with a dying woman?

👄 bittergirlspeak

Let's think long term here. How are you going to continue the chronic illness facade? Are you going to hire a team of actors to masquerade as your doctor, nurse, homeopath adviser, or chemo consultant? Or are you planning to make a miraculous recovery? An extended life of lies upon lies is not an appealing option for any bittergirl. Besides, do you want an unnecessary scar during bikini season?

Justin and Emily had been broken up for a while when she lied and told Him she'd been diagnosed with cancer. As planned, He came back into her life, wanting to support her and be there at the hospital as she underwent a series of important tests. Emily played the martyr and told Him she wanted to go through this with her true friends, her woman friends. Justin respected her wishes but was waiting at her apartment every night when she came home from the hospital. Emily basked in the glow of their newfound love as she returned from her day trips to the spa. One day she was supposedly going in for an MRI to determine the final diagnosis and, caught up in the details of her elaborate story, told Justin that the MRI was on the second floor near the saddest ward in the hospital, the children's ward. Emily played on His sympathy as He held her close. She shed a few tears as her friend Brandy picked her up. Justin was so worried about her He called the hospital and asked to be directed to the MRI unit on the second floor. The receptionist told Him there was no MRI unit on the second floor. The entire floor was dedicated to geriatrics. Emily was busted.

Just Wanna Have Sex

Your sex life was so good. You just know He can't be getting it better anywhere else. So you phone to tell Him that you think you should still get down and dirty. No strings—just sex between friends; you know He doesn't want anything more. You tell Him you've discovered this new sexual freedom that spurns emotional attachments and is just all about physical pleasure. Deep down, you really know that sex is the way to His heart and that once you're doing the deed He'll look into your eyes and everything will be all right again.

👄 bittergirlspeak

This is the closest you'll ever get to feeling like a prostitute. You've already sunk into the abyss, felt that gaping emptiness in your heart. Sex might seem like the answer, but it's guaranteed to knock you down one more step on the ladder of indignity. He's not using His brain to bang you, and isn't that the biggest sex organ of all? He could be under you, over you, and on you, but that still doesn't mean you have His attention.

Marina actually thought she could handle it. She genuinely believed she could have that fabulous sex with Ed and go on getting better and getting over Him—until the night six months after the initial breakup when He whispered to her, as they lay there bathed in postcoital bliss, that He had to get going. His wife was expecting Him at home.

Eddie had neglected to tell her that He'd gotten married since their breakup. He figured that since they were only having emotionally uninvolved sex she didn't need to know she'd become His mistress and was now cheating on a woman she hadn't even known existed. Thanks for the memories, Fast Eddie.

Accidental Wishing

You secretly hope that while skiing with Bob and Carla you'll take a tumble and fracture your leg in three places and that, because He got the car in the separation, He'll become your personal chauffeur. You wish for some kind of freak accident (nothing causing permanent disfigurement) that would land you in the hospital. He'd rush to your bedside to be with you once again. You find yourself standing in the middle of your backyard during a thunderstorm with a twenty-foot metal rod. Every streetcar idling toward you, the shaky scaffolding on the construction site by your office, even that rickety step on your staircase becomes an opportunity to get Him back. As a damsel in distress, how could He not be your knight in shining armor?

💋 bittergirlspeak

Is He worth the pain of a two-inch metal pin in your femur? Would you really rather fry your insides with electricity than be alone? You're a damsel in distress already BECAUSE of HIM. Don't hold out for Him to save you. Besides, chances are HE WON'T. He already dumped you, remember?

L.J. learned the hard way. Sure, she'd idly imagined a terrible wound and how that would bring Him running to her side. But reality hit when the speaker tower collapsed onto her head at her company's annual general meeting and she was laid up for a month with a severe concussion. Who came to her bedside to help her out? Her bestbittergirlfriends, of course. But not a peep from Him. Oh, she heard that He'd heard what had happened and that apparently He said, "Wow, that's really tough." And after a pause, "I hope she's okay." But then He poured another sangria for Sierra, the eighteen-year-old Pilates instructor He'd left L.J. for, and asked if she needed some more sunscreen rubbed on her back.

Ooh, Baby, Baby

You decide your period seems later than usual and call to tell Him you think you might be pregnant. You just want Him to know that you'd let Him be involved in the child's life. Or you've already bought home pregnancy tests and have figured out what chemicals to add to your pee so the swab will say YES, you're having a baby! He always wanted kids. Of course He'll come back to be the father of little baby Angela. And then when He does come back, you'll make sure you get pregnant right quick to seal the deal.

👄 bittergirlspeak

Who are you kidding?! When little Angela is six months old and He decides He can't take the responsibility of being a father and leaves you again, do you think it'll be easier then than it is now? Better to get through the heartache of being left alone than being left alone as a single mother. That time spent tracking your fertility would be better spent tracking your sanity.

Signs

The signs are everywhere and you can't ignore them! His horoscope says He'll soon become conscious of something that's missing in His life. Or when you play the game of if-I-get-beyond-the-intersection-before-the-light-changes-He'll-come-back-to-me, you win every time! Or "your song" has played every time you drive past His house. All signs are saying you're going to get back together!

👄 bittergirlspeak

His horoscope is talking about His hockey jersey that's still at your place or the new Asian balanced fund in His stock portfolio. The intersection game would have the same outcome if you played if-I-get-beyond-the-intersection-before-the-light-changes-He'll-never-come-back-to-me. And honey, "your song" has been playing every time you drive past His house because you have it on repeat on your car stereo. Read the signs as they are, not how you wish them to be. Here's the biggest sign of all—He dumped you! Do you need to see it on a Jumbotron?

Jealous Guy

You have a big event coming up and you know He'll be there. All of a sudden Ralph from the office doesn't repulse you so much. In fact, if he doesn't speak he's pretty hot. The one thing that made Him go berserk in your relationship was seeing you talk or flirt with other guys. Ralph seems confused about the attention you're paying him but is quick to accept your invitation. You slip on that sexy black cocktail dress, you slide into your stilettos, and with Ralph on your arm you make a fashionably late entrance. He will be SO jealous He won't be able to stand it.

👄 bittergirlspeak

Ah . . . so He sees you with Ralph and thinks how great it is that you're getting over this, over Him. He feels He can finally share His exciting news with you about Him and Yvonne and their recent engagement. And woohoo, you get to take Ralph home at the end of the night. That sounds like a brilliant strategy. Hopefully Ralph will tell you more about his caterpillar collection and the new computer program that tracks their mating habits. Couldn't have planned that one better.

Friends, Right?

You decide that cultivating a lasting friendship with Him is way more important than dwelling on the hurt and pain He's caused you. Who cares if He lied to you, who cares if He was a complete asshole, who cares if He made you feel so low and worthless that you didn't know who you were anymore? When He broke up with you He said He valued you and wanted to be friends. You had something really special in that friendship, right at the core of your relationship. How can you throw that all away just because He no longer loves you? Friendship is the essence of life, right? And you think that maybe, just maybe, that friendship will one day blossom again into something more, something deeper.

💋 bittergirlspeak

When someone says "I just want to be friends," they mean one of three things: 1) "I'm saying I just want to be friends because I'm too much of a coward to tell you that I'm not in love with you anymore," 2) "I'm saying I just want to be friends because that's the only way I know you'll let me leave this table and get away from your puffed-up, sniffling face" or 3) "I'm saying I just want to be friends because even though I don't love you anymore I don't want you or anyone else to hate me or think that I'm a bad guy."

Jo found out that being friends wasn't really what she wanted after all when her ex, Ben, confided in her the love He had for the woman He'd met one day in the grocery checkout line. As she sat listening to Him wax eloquent about Grocery Girl's many (many!) virtues she found herself digging her nails into the palm of her hand to keep herself from passing out. Breathing became difficult—she couldn't seem to get any oxygen into her lungs. Finally awakened out of her "Let's be friends" slumber, Jo went home and text-messaged Him that she'd just been asked to go on a business trip to Norway and wouldn't be back for several months, so not to bother calling her until He heard from her that she was back in town. The point is that friendship with an ex isn't possible until you're COMPLETELY over Him. And that doesn't happen until the end of this book.

Stop the Plot!

So . . . STOP THAT PLOTTING RIGHT NOW! If any of these scenarios remotely resemble a thought or behavior pattern you recognize, call your bestbittergirlfriends, grab that vibrator, or go and take a very long walk! It's another of those times when you need to call on the SOS Safety Measures, grab the contents of your Emergency Kit, reread your Contract, and acknowledge that you need a bit of help.

We know it's embarrassing to admit it. It's even shameful. But honey, these strategies to lure Him back crop up in every bittergirl's BBRP. And you can learn from the collective experience of bittergirls everywhere that NO, NONE OF THESE THINGS WILL WORK!

The first step to veering off this path of disgrace—and *disgrace* is a gracious word for it—is to admit that you're scheming to get Him back. The longer you deny it, the more painful it'll be in the long run.

You see, you could change every little thing about you that you think caused the breakup, but honey, YOU are not the reason the two of you broke up. HE is the reason. Plotting to get Him back can be fun, it can help while away the hours, it can afford you daydreams of happiness and a potential future. But ask yourself this: *Do you really want to plot to get someone back?*

bittergirls who didn't plot (and look where they are now)

Alanis Morissette

Way to have your revenge and a gazillion-selling album too, baby! Alanis never named names in *Jagged Little Pill,* so no one got hurt, it was all very classy, and she's become the unofficial anthem to many a breakup.

Hillary Rodham Clinton

Oh, she had reason to plot and fume, but she just got on with it and ran for the Senate. Enough said.

Nicole Kidman

It's not just our imagination: She would never have won the Oscar if she were still schlepping around in flats trying to look shorter than Tom.

Nora Ephron

Here's a woman we like: Get cheated on and use the material for a fabulous novel and then watch your screenwriting and directing career take off making the romantic movies we all swoon for. *Sleepless in Seattle* is one of our bittergirl favorites.

Is He Really Such a Prize?

At this point we'd like to address a certain phrase that a lot of people seem to be brandishing nowadays. "Nine strategies to *win back* the love of your life." "*Win him back* in ninety days or less." "How to use all I learned at my Ivy League university to *win him back.*" WIN HIM BACK? Is He really such a prize? If He were, He wouldn't have dumped you in the first place! And really, if He did come back, are you the one who's winning?

Okay, let's just say one of these plots has worked and you have Him back. He's moved back in, His stuff is out of the boxes, your names come up together on caller ID. Now what? Do you think what he disliked about you when He dumped you has suddenly changed? Will Engagement Probation turn into Honeymoon Probation, Pregnancy Probation, Second Child Probation—or have you just accepted the fact that you're on Permanent Probation?

All those problems you had before your relationship ended aren't just going to go away. They're like a running injury. If you rest and don't run, the injury may miraculously disappear and you might find yourself feeling no pain. But if you don't address the problem that caused the injury in the first place, the moment you start running again you're going to reinjure yourself and it will feel WORSE. Why would your relationship be any different?

Take Eva, who feigned her own spleenectomy. After all, who can tell whether you've got a spleen or not? Eva really thought she'd pulled it off. Her ex was so supportive and nursed her back to health. He'd spent days researching the operation and how it would affect Eva and her life. And when He thought she was strong enough to take the news, He told her He'd developed a "special friendship" with a woman He met while attending the Spleenectomy Family Support Group.

Think about the reality of your situation. If instead of plotting to get Him back you told Him right now the plain truth—that you still love Him and want to get back together—would He come? What would His answer be? Be honest with yourself. If it's No, do you really want that to change out of guilt, pity, or obligation?

A bittergirl does not need to diminish herself. Plus, if He did come back as a result of your trickery, do you think you'd be able to relax right back into a loving and happy relationship? How would you feel knowing He was with you for the wrong reasons? And would you have to keep on plotting to keep Him there? Where does it end? Remember that old saying: Relationships built on lies are like castles built on sand.

It all comes back to self-respect and what you deserve. Hold on to your dignity—wrap it around you and wear it like a cloak. You're a bittergirl in training, and while duping Him back into your life may feel good momentarily, at the end of the day you'll be the one who's been conned.

bitteractivities

1. Wear It Out. . . .   Put on the outfit you were wearing the night He dumped you. And don't lie, of course you remember what you were wearing. Recall the feeling. Do you think anything will change if you "win" Him back?

2. Change the Plot   Write a plot to get *yourself* back. It's all about where you put your energies.

3. Bulletproof Your Foolproof Plan   You know and we know there's no such thing as a foolproof plan. BUT if you insist on going through with any of these crazy schemes, make sure you know down to every nitty-gritty detail how it's going to work. Watch movies with bank heists, mysterious murders, mistaken identities, and medical dramas. In those movies the hero always has a trusty sidekick who's an expert in the field. Who's your sidekick going to be? Hopefully by the time your research is done you'll have calmed down a bit and you'll be able to entertain your BBGFs later with your zany tale. Either that or you have a new career as a screenwriter.

eleven

bittersweet revenge

"I WISH HE WAS DEAD." We know, honey, and we do too. But the fact of the matter is He's not dead. In fact, He's alive and well and probably taking His pecker out on a little vacation.

Oh, our fabulous fledgling bittergirl. You've been through a lot in the last little while. The rug was pulled out from under you, and you've cried, you've mourned, you've been busy picking up the pieces of your wounded soul. But these days you're not so sad anymore, not so stunned and immobile, and a new emotion is beginning to percolate through your veins. What is that—we don't recognize it—could it be . . . anger? Why yes, we believe it is. And with that anger, something else seems to be bubbling up, a thought that can't be pushed away, can't be dismissed. Wait, it's forming slowly, it's taking shape through the mists of your conscious being, it's . . . Revenge.

There comes a time after every breakup when there's nothing a bittergirl would like better than to wreak revenge on the One Who's Done Her Wrong. But how do you actually avenge the death of a relationship? By what means do you retaliate after a humiliating public dump courtesy of the man you were just beginning to open up to?

What could possibly be harsh enough punishment to mete out after the meltdown of a marriage?

Revenge stories are funny, screamingly funny in a can't-take-your-eyes-off-that-train-wreck kind of way. They're tales from the dark side. Everybody knows about the cousin of a friend who talked her way into a catering uniform to stalk her ex at a family bat mitzvah. The companion at the gym who left her silky undergarments under His pillow for the Other Woman to find. The sister who fell off His fire escape in her break-and-enter attempt and spent three days in hospital. The bittergirls even know one fabulous woman whose ex was famously proud of His luscious locks of hair. When she found out He was cheating on her she began quietly diluting His shampoo with Nair until He eventually went to His doctor, so concerned was He about His suddenly thinning mane.

Now, bittergirls are not addicted to drama; we've had it thrust upon us. Certainly everyone likes a little excitement in her world, but most of us like living happily ever after. We tend to prefer to have our theatrics in novels and in movies starring Colin Firth or Cary Grant. So if our budding bittergirl is living for revenge, if her waking hours are becoming consumed with thoughts of how exactly she's going to carry it out, then it is time to pause and reflect.

Equally, bittergirls are not mean-spirited. Everyone needs to get the bile out of her system at some point in her life, and fantasy is a fabulous way of doing that. But when fantasy starts to take over reality and you find yourself actually plotting the details of your revenge, you're stepping dangerously close to the line, honey. The sisterhood is here to tell you: Put that key down and step *away* from that finely polished finish of His brand-new car.

Here you stand, trying to talk civilly to Steve about who has the rights to that lovely leather club chair. Yes, that's right, the one you bought together a year ago on that sunny Saturday afternoon at your favorite furniture store uptown. You were so happy! Lattes in hand, arms wrapped affectionately around each other . . . Steve whips out His calculator and you snap back to the present. As He proceeds to figure out the depreciated value of said leather chair after a year's use in your shared domicile, you eye the quivering two-foot icicle hanging like the Sword of Damocles over His head. And there's a piece of you that truly believes that if it were to suddenly, conveniently, fall and impale Him, His lips still mouthing inanities and His fingers still tapping at the calculator, you would truly be a happier person. But you wouldn't. And in a little while from now you'll be able to talk to Steve about the furniture you once owned together and not want to back over Him with the moving van He's hired with your credit card.

That said, there is a place in every breakup and recovery for a little vengeful fantasizing. You've been treated badly by one whom you loved, or one whom you hoped to love, and that deserves a few guilt-free bad thoughts. The key words here are *few* and *thoughts*.

Top Three Most Popular Revenge Strategies

Bunny Boiling

Yes, you want to know everything He's been doing. And it's difficult to understand how the man who called you four times a day at the office "just to check in" suddenly doesn't want to give you the time of day. Sure, you might be compelled to set up surveillance cameras around His house, infiltrate His squash league, or send Him a virus to disable His BlackBerry.

Resist the urge. None of this will make you feel any better. If you do plug in to those cameras, all you'll discover is that He's going on with His life as before. Or, worse, that He's having a better time than He was with you. Odds are that you've imagined He's crazy; that He's lost His mind somehow and will eventually come back to His senses.

Once you see Him wandering through the streets of town in His pajamas and a dirty trenchcoat you'll run to Him and rescue Him and He'll fall into your arms, weeping with relief and crying, "Oh my God I thought I had lost you forever—what was I thinking please please take me back I beg of you my darling. . . ." Honey, it ain't gonna happen.

Holly was a bunny boiler. She shadowed Him day and night. When she found Him with His arm around a comely new friend at the restaurant He and Holly had frequented together, she pulled the fire alarm. She was shocked to be barred from the restaurant for life and charged with public mischief. Resist the urge. Phone up your bestbittergirlfriends and let them talk you down. A good risotto is hard to find.

Damage to His Property

Hmm, dicey. Burning the smaller belongings He left behind in a sensible spot like your fireplace or Hibachi is one thing: There's a certain symbolic something about that and it can tangibly satisfy your need for revenge. But vandalizing His home or car is way over the line and can lead to nasty criminal charges. Cars are strangely important to many boys, and so it follows that vehicles have been known to mysteriously roll unaided into a ditch after being left in neutral. Some bad-acting ex-boyfriends have tried to start their cars in the morning only to find sugar in their gas tanks. Windshields have been broken, finishes destroyed, antennae snapped . . . you get the picture. Getting caught at any of these activities could get you landed in your local courtroom. And wouldn't you be happier having your nails done with your best friend than spending the afternoon pleading your case with a bunch of lawyers? They aren't all as empathetic and easy to talk to as Sam Waterston.

Magda found out that her husband was cheating on her with the Office Bitch, the one who had made all their honeymoon travel arrangements, had shared her real estate agent with them, had even picked up their sons from hockey every once in a while. Magda figured her ex-husband would need some of His stuff for His new condo, so she packed everything she thought He could use into two big cardboard boxes, placed them at the bottom of their drive, and with a big black marker wrote ADULTERER across them. She called to tell them that His stuff was ready and that He could pick it up at any time. Unfortunately He couldn't come until later that night, He said. Magda said "No problem." As it turned out, He didn't come till the next morning, so everyone in their neighborhood had a chance to see who He really was.

Magda is happily living in the same house with her two sons. She makes her own travel arrangements, and she picks her boys up from hockey every night. Magda and the fellow bittergirls in her neighborhood have breakfast together every Tuesday.

Trashing His Reputation

Allegra told us over mojitos of choosing a few lewd photos of her ex from her personal album and uploading them to various porn sites . . . funny in theory but far, far over the line for a dignified bittergirl. Ditto for the woman who got hold of the videos of her ex and His new squeeze making the beast with two backs and showed it at a Super Bowl party as the pregame entertainment. Putting up posters with His phone number and "For a good time call . . . 24/7!" is far too much effort for a pastime far too illegal. And you know what? Making that phone call to the tax department on their anonymous snitch line is just a little too cruel. We know one bittergirl who worked for the government and flagged her ex's income tax. His life has never been the same: She's been over Him for years now, but He's living through the hell of His third audit as we speak.

A cardinal rule to live by: Do not go to His mother. Do not trash Him to His mother. Do not pour out your heart to His mother. She may have been the most loving mother-in-law in the world. She may have welcomed you into her heart and home. She may have recognized you as the daughter she never had. But when it all comes down to it, SHE IS HIS MOTHER. She gave birth to Him. She raised Him. She loves Him more than she loves you. Even if she agrees with you about every horrible thing He did to you, guess what? He is the fruit of her loins. He wins. He always will. And don't try to befriend His sister, His uncle, anyone else in His family. You may have swapped bodily fluids, you may even have given birth to His child, but they are blood and you are not. They're on His side of the fence. Enough with the toxicity. You can trash His reputation safely and have a few laughs at His expense with your bestbittergirlfriends and still come out of it with a cordial relationship with His family, whom you may have loved despite the fact that they raised this dysfunctional son.

Staking the Moral High Ground

Drinks in hand at a corner table in your neighborhood bistro, tales of Sarah-Jane-from-the-corner-office slashing the art in her ex's home may seem pretty funny. But after an evening's delicious contemplation, any right-thinking bittergirl will shake her head and recognize that, whew, she dodged a bullet there. Thank God *I* didn't do anything like that.

Now, every bittergirl has had the odd little lapse in judgment. But when you get right down to it, acting on your revenge instincts is Not a Good Thing. People refer to "revenge fantasies" for a reason: They are, and should remain, *fantasies*. No bittergirl wants to wake up in a holding cell. Fodder for the next chapter of your as-yet-unpublished autobiographical novel it may be, but in the grand scheme of things, it's not any bittergirl's ideal choice of overnight accommodation. And frankly, a police record is commonly looked upon as a blot on the copybook of life.

practical revenges

1. Return the toothbrush He left at your place, but make sure you clean the toilet with it first.

2. Return that best-selling thriller He left sitting beside your bed, but cut out the final three pages before you do.

3. March yourself right into the bank and cancel that joint account. Consult the lawyer.

4. Clean out the drawers and gather His stuff. Take it to a consignment store. Still hasn't picked up His guitar? Take it to a pawn shop. At least you'll stand to gain a profit.

5. Don't bother returning His fabulous cappuccino machine. If He hasn't picked it up by now, we think you deserve a great cup of your favorite java in the mornings. The spoils of war, baby.

6. Don't forward His mail. He's a big boy. He'll get around to changing His address when His telephone is cut off in three months. In the meantime, it's not your problem.

7. Have your engagement ring melted down and redesigned as a pair of classy earrings for yourself. Better yet, hold on to them for your daughter.

8. Buy yourself that car you and He could never afford. Make sure all His friends see you in it.

9. He always hated your friends Marj and Benedict. Buy them season tickets next to His at the opera.

10. Get over Him.

Dignity, Always Dignity

The bittergirls have heard the stories, oh, have we heard the stories. Lisa resorted to the oldie but goodie of sending a million magazine subscriptions to His address. Cat left flyers on every windshield in His office and apartment parking lot detailing His evil ways. Another approach is to e-mail everybody in your mutual address book with your rebuttal to the breakup, or simply to CC His cyberdump to the world or post it on His office chat board. Ah, the number of e-mails the bittergirls have received of this juicy nature. It's quick and it's effective. But it can also broadcast your own pain and momentary instability to the world—and is that really how you want the world to see you?

Tilley, a charter bittergirl, spent several months plotting how she could sneak back into His apartment and short-circuit His precious surround-sound home theater system. Until her blinding moment of clarity, that is, when she realized that she didn't want to look back in her dotage at a year's worth of journal entries entirely about Him and How She Would Wreak Revenge. So put your life back into perspective: Three years from now, do you want to recollect with a maidenly blush the night you egged His house? Wouldn't you prefer to remember this as the time you discovered what a great friend Christina was to you and how you began planning your first annual February girls-only trip to the tropics?

Not being big on criminal behavior and its attendant lack of decorum, we prefer the restrained yet imaginative response to the dump. These are the satisfying, creative revenges that hurt no one and restore a bit of your wounded pride. Jenet, for example, simply snipped a thread in His three-hundred-dollar cashmere sweater and waited quietly for it to unravel.

The bittergirls cannot say it too often: There's a time and a place for acting out, but for the most part those funny revenge stories are best enjoyed as cautionary tales. A bittergirl's advantage in life is her dignity: Use it as your shield for the duration of your Bittergirl Breakup Recovery Period.

This may also be the time when you begin to wonder if maybe it's the drama you're addicted to and not, after all, your ex. And what does that say about you? Is your life really so unoccupied that you can afford to waste it on someone like Him? Because no one, believe us, *no one* is worth that amount of time and energy. This is your life, and you'll never get this moment back again. If you'd expended the same amount of effort plotting your career as you did your revenge, you'd be the CEO of a multinational corporation. And wouldn't that ultimately be a sweeter revenge than any petty thing you could do to Him or His stuff?

Deny, Deny, Deny

We keep telling you, sweetheart, don't do it. Don't act it out—you're worth more than Him. But even we have to admit that sometimes it does feel really, really good. So let's say you *have* acted it out. You've done whatever you wanted to do in your worst imaginings. You've listened to our bittergirl tales of outrageous behavior and thought to yourself, "That's nothing." Fine. It's done. The bittergirls are here to say *give up on guilt*. If you've done it, let it go and move on. And you know from bittergirl experience that what we're saying is true.

Sometimes a bittergirl will lose her head; sometimes a bittergirl will indulge in behavior that she knows won't look good down the road; sometimes she just stays at the party a little too long and things get ugly. So when someone asks you if you were there, if you had a hand in it, if you know what happened, take the bittergirls' advice. Look them straight in the eye, toss your hair, look faintly puzzled, and repeat after us: "No, I wasn't there. No, I left early. No, I went straight home. . . ." Not advocated when questioned by the authorities, but for the minor infractions in life, denial can effectively shut down those busybodies who only want the dirt. Someday you can admit to being there when the strip poker got down to the bare necessities, when the police arrived, when the bottles were drained and the cooking sherry came out, when everyone shucked their clothing and dove into the neighbor's pool . . . but not now. So smile and shake your head slightly and say, "No, I left at eight o'clock—why? What happened?"

Bittergirls Know When to Say When

Imagine how good you'll look when you see Him next. Imagine how good you'll feel when you're sitting in the window of that restaurant He always hated and you always loved, when He walks by just as you're laughing at the funny thing your bestbittergirlfriend said. He's outside the loop, outside your world, and it's a world you love and are comfortable in. And with time, you could even run into Him when you're wearing sweatpants and it's Saturday evening and you're on your way to pick up your dry cleaning. He'll still look after you and think, "Wow, what did I lose when I lost her?" Because if you take care of your own self and get your soul back under your own control, you'll have your life back in order. And that shows in your eyes, your voice, the way you carry yourself, and in every aspect of your life.

The bittergirls know. The first February after they met and bonded, they had a Valentine's dinner for themselves. The victims of many a breakup, they were all single at the time and nursing bruised egos, so they decided to celebrate themselves with a fantastic meal and much red wine. Who better to spend Valentine's with than the ones who love you—and that should include your own fine self. You have to take care of the most important person in your life sometimes, and that's the person who so often gets lost in the shuffle. Treat yourself. Treat your friends.

Sure, crazy, vengeful behavior may be instantaneously gratifying, but the bittergirls are here to remind you that it's like drinking—that first sip will make the world feel warm and cozy, but wake up in the cold light of day with an aching head and a furry mouth and you'll know you should never have drunk the whole bottle. Bittergirls know how to say when. When you're feeling whole and strong again (and you will be—believe us, you will be), look back on a journal entry from the time you were hurting the most or go into an Internet chat room and read postings from women hell-bent on revenge: You'll shake your head not in recognition but in disbelief. As any woman who's given birth will tell you, Nature protects us from pain by letting us forget it.

Besides, after a while such contortions do try the bonds of the bittergirl sorority. "Why, without the help of a martini shaker it was difficult to sit through Mitzi's call to action for the fourteenth time last Thursday," one bittergirl might say to another. "What," says a third, "is she still tracking down those architect's plans for Rolf's building to plan her escape route after she performs The Great Humiliation?" Three stylish bittergirl heads nod, three dainty little yawns are stifled, and the conversation moves on to far more fascinating topics, such as World Domination by Bittergirls Everywhere, and have you tried that new Australian Cabernet yet?

Breakups are painful—but hell, *life* is painful. You're a big brave girl: Remind yourself once again of all you've endured in your life. You made it through that downsizing at work; you got through all those Christmas dinners with Aunt Agnes and the kids; you got through Cousin Lou's endless seder. For God's sake, you made it through high school! You can get through a breakup, and you can do it without resorting to tactics that'll make one's toes curl up in squeamish recollection.

The Sweetest Bittergirl Revenge

Nothing will make Him want you more than your being healthy and strong and not needing Him. He wooed you in the beginning—you weren't imagining it. Then for whatever reasons the partnership changed, the relationship ended, and He didn't want you. It hurt— oh God, how it hurt. But now you've moved on and avenged the breakup in myriad ways that He couldn't possibly comprehend. You bought that club membership and have the satisfaction of using it when you want to, not because He said, "Well, are you going to waste money on another gym you'll never use after the first month *again?*" Or you stayed up till four in the morning in your own cozy bed reading that great new Helen Fielding novel right through to the end while munching cheese and crackers, without having to listen to Him sigh and toss and turn and say, "Are you ever going to turn out the light?" Or you finally started up that business on your own that He thought was too risky. Or you took that Russian literature class that He always implied (always affectionately!) was slightly beyond your pretty little head.

So now He sees you on the street as you run for that cab in your fabulous new shoes after your Thursday evening yoga class to dart off to a get-together with your new friends from your restaurant appreciation group—guess what? You get to be truly polite and removed and disinterested because you're moving on with your life. You've cultivated more self-respect than to go running back to someone who's already rejected you. Because you're worth more than that— you're special. You are unique. And you should be with someone who wants you as much as you want him. It's a partnership, honey, and He bailed. So ultimately He did you a favor because, sweetie, you deserve better. Every bittergirl knows it is true.

♟ bitteractivities

1. Your Ultimate Revenge   Imagine the worst thing you could do to Him: your Ultimate Revenge. Now describe it in gory detail— write it out and put it away. At least two hours later, invite your bestbittergirlfriend over and get her to read it to you as if it were her story. Then get her to read it again. After the laughter stops, think long and hard. How would you talk her down from doing this heinous thing? What's it going to do to her life? Will it give her a few moments of satisfaction in exchange for a jail sentence or a lifetime reputation? What would you say to her? Talk her out of it and then take a moment and listen to your own advice.

Then open a bottle of your favorite beverage, pour out a bowl of your favorite snack, and together let your fantasies run free. Talk them out until you can imagine nothing else, say goodnight, and go to sleep free of the bile you've been carrying with you.

Like your favorite shrink, the bittergirls are here to remind you that there's nothing worse than the unspoken—it festers in your brain and spurts out at the most untoward moments. You have to give voice to that bitterness and let yourself enjoy it. You don't need to act on it—just give it a voice. Only then can you laugh about it and move on.

2. Embrace Your Anger (Punch It Out)   Feeling violent? No way around it and no way to get it out? Punch that punching bag. You know, the one with His face on it? Or join a kickboxing class.

3. Create a Ritual   Okay, you can't get past the feeling of wanting to do something unreasonable and out of control. So create a ritual and keep the actual violence to a minimum. Invite a friend over and make it into a cleansing ceremony. Cut His head out of your favorite picture of the two of you together, burn it, then toast your newfound freedom. Find something of His that He left behind and perform the violence on it, not Him. Share how you're feeling with your friend. And to reward her for her patience, take yourselves somewhere nice for the evening. It can be a posh restaurant, a cozy coffee shop, or a fantastic potluck dinner at home by candlelight—but do something for yourself and your pal to celebrate your psychic victory.

4. Make *Yourself* Your Hobby   What were the things you did for Him every day? Try doing a little of that for yourself. Find a few concrete examples and do one or two of them for yourself daily. How did you help Him along in His life and career? Did you encourage Him and try to make Him feel better about Himself? How about doing the same for you? If it's hard to pat yourself on the back, get together with your most encouraging and supportive friends and make sure you get a little of the TLC that you lavished on Him. How much time did you give to Him and your relation-ship? Give that gift of time to yourself. One bittergirl says that at the end of her marriage she lamented the fact that His career was so much farther ahead than hers, until she realized that she'd been concentrating on Him for the past seven years. She gave herself the same amount of time to support herself emotionally and psychologically the same way, and lo and behold, seven years later she was indeed doing as well in her career as He'd been when He left her. Seven years might seem like a long time, but you can count the short-term milestones along the way—and celebrate them with the bittergirls.

5. Fantasize the Best Possible You   Imagine the best possible way you could look, what you could be doing, how you could act when you next see Him. Figure out three different scenarios. Make them as detailed as possible and write down your favorite. Seal it in an envelope and put it in your drawer. When you DO actually see Him next, write down exactly how you felt or call another bittergirl to let it all out. Keep doing this until the day comes when, eureka! you don't need to anymore. Because you saw Him, and you didn't really care how you felt or what He thought. That will be the day He calls *His* best friend to tell him how great you looked when He saw you. And that's the day you'll truly be free of Him.

twelve
bittergirl breakdown

YOU'VE FANTASIZED ABOUT YOUR REVENGE and maybe even acted out a little portion of it, you've cleansed your apartment of Him, you've cut Him out of all your pictures, you've painted Him out of your life. You're starting to get the hang of this and are resembling a sane human being once more. This is working. You're feeling like a bittergirl. You sign your name "one of the BGs," your bestbittergirlfriends are family to you now, you're always concerned about KUA. You even feel safe venturing out without your team. Look at you go! You're whole; you know you're better off without Him. You've accepted the Warning Signs you missed and you're moving forward with your life. You feel sexy and confident and full of possibility.

And WHAM! Suddenly you find yourself straddling him, screaming sexual exclamations you've never even heard before, and riding him like a mechanical bull. How did you get here, you ask? A moment of weakness hit and you acted on it. Welcome to the Bittergirl Breakdown.

You were coping so well. You held it together when He bought your half of the car. You held it together while divvying up the furniture. There were no tears when you divided the photographs. Your team helped you move into your new loft apartment on the hottest day of the year, the freight elevator broke down and you did not crack. You have spackled in holes, killed mice, hooked up your DVD player, and there have been no scenes.

Until the night you go to the all-night hardware store. There you are at 3 A.M. roaming the aisles, buggy full of screwdrivers and drill bits and low-wattage lightbulbs, because you are learning about all this stuff now, and you get to the paint section. You go through the paint chips but after a while all the shades of blue start to look the same. You ask the guy at the counter what shade he thinks is the closest to cobalt and suddenly the reality of your life sinks in. You are asking some pockmarked eighteen-year-old what color to paint your kitchen. You are not creating a home together, you and young Zach, you are not riding off into the sunset. Yet here you are pleading with this stranger, this child, this skater punk for some guidance, some strength, some sorry lady I know your life wasn't always like this, some no lady we get women in here at 3 A.M. sobbing all the time, some no you aren't crazy, some just tell me what shade of goddamned blue this is!!!! He mixes what you both think is cobalt. He's a teenager. He should be home in bed, he probably has school tomorrow. Instead he throws his ten-speed in the back of your car and you have sex with him in your soon-to-be-cobalt kitchen.

We first talked about moments of weakness in Chapter 4. They're a rite of passage for every bittergirl: the immediate, desperate pleas for a ride to back-together-land, the yearning to grasp why this is happening, the frantic clambering to pick up the pieces and reattach them. You discovered your survival techniques (with a little help from the bittergirls). The Emergency Kit, the Safety Measures, and the Contract became your lifelines as you took your first few steps away from The Incident. And then again you faced the demons of Him as you mythologized your relationship and were beguiled by the notion of getting Him back.

You endured all this with your bittergirl pride intact. It's hard not to feel infallible. But once you've navigated these dark terrains, don't fall into the trap of believing you can forgo BBRP procedures. It is just this false sense of security that leads to momentary failures in judgment. The minute you let your vigilance lapse, the mechanical bull rides on in.

ten ways to tell you've had a bittergirl breakdown

1. You've left twenty-eight messages on His voicemail this morning and are contemplating the twenty-ninth.

2. You've decided that memorizing every line of *Who's Afraid of Virginia Woolf?* will help you in your affairs of the heart.

3. You're finishing your sixth step class in a row, taking a breather only to check your messages.

4. You're at your computer and you've just programmed your Instant Messenger setting to read "I'm turned on and ready to go."

5. You're at a local sports bar (without your bestbittergirl-friends) drinking Jägermeister and telling your story to the local rugby team.

6. You've invited yourself to His parents' place for Sunday dinner in hopes that He'll happen to show up.

7. You've been at the local karaoke bar for eight hours and you keep singing "I Want You to Want Me" by Cheap Trick.

8. You've paid the Jumbotron controller at the nearest sports arena to display the words "Jeff, I can't live if living is without you."

9. You're at His cousin's wedding as His ten-year-old nephew's date.

10. You're creating a scrapbook of your relationship to mark what would have been your five-year anniversary.

Don't cringe, darling. You may think the Bittergirl Breakdown is the last thing anyone could ever pay you to do right now, but as The Bittergirl Institute for Advanced Research on Dumping has found, 98 percent of bittergirls have crashed and burned at some point. If you're in the remaining 2 percent, check your pulse and, if it's still throbbing, give yourself a hearty pat on the back for being ramrod strong and skip to the next chapter. On second thought, maybe you should read this anyway, just in case. . . .

For the other 98 percent of bittergirls, the road to hell is paved with good intentions, but that hairline fracture of vulnerability we talked about in Chapter 4 has just become a bottomless chasm of pent-up loneliness, sexual need, anger, misery, frustration, and desire.

Now there's something you should know about Bittergirl Breakdowns. THEY COME OUT OF NOWHERE. When the breakdown occurs you're usually far beyond the Plotting to Get Him Back stage. You probably laugh at how silly all those scheming thoughts were. "How could I have sunk so low?" you might ask. You snicker at the idea of revenge. "Why would I waste my time?"

👄 bittergirlspeak

Bittergirl Breakdowns sneak up on you, catch you unaware, utterly blindside you, then leave you reeling the next day wondering who you are and how you got here. Hmm, reminiscent somewhat of how you felt after The Incident? In a way, yes, but the beauty of the Bittergirl Breakdown is that you already have all the equipment to deal with it and you're in control. Bittergirl reminder: You do know who you are and you do know how you got here.

A Bittergirl Breakdown is really a big, stupid moment of weakness. The key word to focus on here is *MOMENT*. You see, the moment is over, the breakdown happened. How it happened means nothing at this point in time. But how you react to it means everything.

Common Bittergirl Breakdowns

Reunion Sex

This is the most common of Bittergirl Breakdowns. You bump into Him in the weirdest of places (and it's been months since you stalked Him), and you both seem genuinely happy to see each other. You chat for a bit and decide to have tea, coffee, a drink. The next thing you know you're laughing like old times, you're finishing each other's sentences, you're staring longingly into each other's eyes. All these feelings are welling up inside you, and you can see He's feeling them too. And, and, and . . . well, one thing leads to another and you end up doing the nasty in His bed, on the kitchen counter, on a park bench, in the backseat of His brand-new Saab. ("Oh, don't stain the leather!")

During reunion sex you may be caught up in the lust of it all, the passion brought on by your eighth gin and tonic, the way His collarbone curves to meet His shoulder, the comfort of His voice, of knowing His body. You may feel like this is the right thing, that you're invincible as you become the star of His rodeo. But ask yourself this: *How will I feel in twenty-four hours?* This is a good rule to live by when it comes to Bittergirl Breakdowns.

Melissa bumped into Grant at a bar one night after work (a true coincidence—neither of them had ever been to that bar before). He looked fabulous, she looked fabulous, they had a few drinks and started reminiscing. He told her He was no longer with the neighbor's daughter, that He knew it never would have lasted. He bought Melissa a rose from the flower man ("The first time He'd EVER bought me a flower," she told us), and before long they were cabbing it home, barely keeping their hands off each other. While having the rowdiest sex ever, Grant kept saying, "What are you doing? This isn't like you." Melissa was beside herself. "Yes it is baby. This is me. In touch and on top. Does baby like it like this? Did the NEIGHBOR'S DAUGHTER do it like this?" Apparently Grant didn't like it like that because two weeks later He still hadn't returned Melissa's phone call.

Reunion sex is familiar territory for a lot of bittergirls. We've learned that it's best to address it, pull yourself together, touch up your mascara, brush out that bed head, and keep moving forward. Celebrate the fact that you just got laid. Don't dwell on the fact that you got laid by Him, the one you've been trying to get over.

The critical issue here is to BE REALISTIC ABOUT IT. If you're holding on to a glimmer of hope that this one night of passion means the path to back-together-land, let the bittergirls remind you of who it was you just slept with. What was the name you gave Him? The Coward? The Mountie? Missing in Action? Magic Man? Yes, well, He's still That Guy. He's just now That-Guy-who-couldn't-resist-sleeping-with-you-again. Did He tell you why He slept with you? Was it just because He could?

As charter bittergirl Susan discovered, Rick had sex with her one more time just to make sure His new girlfriend was "the one." The next day, while she was busy making plans for Him to move back in, He was making his girlfriend his fianceé.

Or take Andrea, who was daydreaming of the date she and Tom made for the following night when her secretary handed her a FedEx parcel. In it were the birth control pills she'd accidentally left in His bathroom and a note that said, "I hope you're okay. I don't want to mess up your process. I just felt like you really needed me last night. I'm off to India tomorrow and won't be back for a while." Andrea coined it a "pity fuck" and it was the last time she saw Tom, ever.

Then there's Meredith, whose horoscope had told her that something great was going to happen. When she slept with Raymond again, she thought He was that "great thing." Until He accidentally sat on His cell phone the following night and speed-dialed her number. As Raymond recounted the crazy-ass sex with His crazy-ass ex to His pal Joey, Meredith listened in horror. Her horoscope for that day said to reevaluate her position on things, and she definitely did.

The Family Meltdown

It's a beautiful spring day. You're out shopping, enjoying the sunshine, basking in the glow of your new fabulous self when you feel a tap on your shoulder. You turn around and no, it couldn't be? It is. It's His mother. You haven't seen her since The Incident. She misses you. You were such a big part of the family. They all wish they'd had a chance to say goodbye. She gives you a big hug. The next thing you know your tear ducts have turned on full blast, you're spluttering and snotty, you can't seem to string a sentence together. "I . . . I . . . mi . . . miss . . . Hi . . . Hi . . . m . . . so . . . sooo . . . mu . . . much" (heave, sob). She takes you by the hand and sits you down on the hood of the nearest car until you calm down forty-five minutes later. She offers you a ride home and you decline, saying you're meeting a friend in ten minutes just around the corner. She hugs you goodbye and you crawl to the nearest alley and crumple into your shopping bags.

How could this happen? You thought you were doing so well. Honey, this was one of those sucker punches we've been talking about. Give yourself some credit. If you could have seen it coming, you would have ducked.

The bittergirls want to remind you that this is what it is: a MOMENT of weakness. The moment has passed, thank God, and it's behind you. You'll never have to go through that exact scenario again. Phew. You could spend the next twenty-four hours worrying about whether she'll tell Him and how foolish you'd feel, but why bother? If she's going to tell Him, she's going to tell Him—and so what? You had a mini meltdown, but it's just more fodder for the fantastically funny tale you'll be telling years from now. The point is, get over it right now. You can't do anything about what His mom does. You *can* do something about what you do. Call your bestbittergirlfriends and cry-laugh as you relay the story.

Monica bumped into His parents at a black-tie charity function she helped organize. They always looked so stylish and sophisticated; she felt frumpy and out of place. She thought they'd never liked her and was surprised when they fawned over her in front of their snobby friends. They insisted she join them at their table after dinner. To calm her nerves her friend Ellie kept refilling her wineglass. Three hours later Monica was slumped at their table, slurring her words, admonishing them for raising such a selfish, horrid, heartless son. The next morning Ellie called to see if she remembered anything. Monica didn't know what she was talking about. Ellie kept the information to herself until a few months later. (Now that's a bestbittergirlfriend for you.)

Making Contact

This breakdown is often prompted by special occasions. Have you ever noticed how a birthday, a national holiday, any celebratory event tends to bring up emotions you thought were long buried? Your friend Mandy calls to remind you of the baby shower you're supposed to go to. You suddenly realize that tomorrow is His best friend's wedding, His mother's retirement party is less than a month away, His younger brother's art exhibit is this afternoon, His boss's baby is due in three weeks. You're inundated with smells, sounds, sights that remind you of Him; nostalgic feelings overwhelm you. Your sanity slips away as you begin your little tap dance down memory lane. And you find yourself in one of the following scenarios.

The Letter   It's the day you always used to fly to Florida for the holidays. You write a tear-stained letter to His mother: "Hi [sniffle], how are you? What are you doing for Hanukkah? [snuffle] Going to Florida? Oh [heaving sobs] . . . I love Florida. . . ."

The Phone Call   You hold Him hostage on the phone, threatening to jump off the ledge of your bedroom window if He doesn't come back to you. He reminds you that you live on the first floor.

Message Sent   You wake up hungover after your boss's engagement party and when you check your e-mail you see that you sent Him a message marked urgent at 2:32 A.M. The title of the e-mail was "It's S&M week. How about some bondage, baby?" OH MY GOD.

I'm Here!   You're standing at the back of the church and an usher asks you which side you're with—the bride's or the groom's? You don't belong to either. It's His cousin's wedding and you actually weren't invited.

This breakdown is usually motivated by your overwhelming desire to fit back into your old life. But let us remind you, it's your *old* life. As you well know by now, the rules of disengagement have changed all your boundaries, and these rules apply here. Even if you went to

His best friend's engagement party together, you cannot go to the wedding. You might have helped plan His mother's retirement party, but you've got to hand over the itinerary to someone else. In the judgment lapse that leads to this Bittergirl Breakdown you become convinced that if you just initiate contact with Him or His family you can show yourself you're over Him. But honey, you're being delusional. You're not quite there yet.

Take it from Imogen, who suffered a severe case of Bittergirl Breakdown: "It was the book launch for our friend Mark's new Spanish travel book; we were all supposed to be there, all of Mark's friends, and that included me and my ex, Matthew. I had the door to the house open all that day and I kept seeing all our neighbors and friends walking down the street to the neighborhood bookstore where it was happening. Finally I couldn't stand it anymore and I got dressed and I went. Matthew would be there but so what? I was a grown woman. I could handle it. Matthew was the first person I saw. He was talking to Mark's wife. I was incredibly uncomfortable so I downed a couple of glasses of complimentary sangria and then a few more. I have a vague memory of interrupting Mark's reading with the tale of that time in Madrid when Matthew couldn't get it up. Apparently they stuffed tapas in my mouth to shut me up. Mark's father walked me home and I woke up at 4 A.M. in the deck chair on my front porch." Ouch.

When Stacey called her ex to meet for a quiet Christmas drink more than a year after her breakup, she believed it was completely safe. She felt like she was flourishing in her new life. It was the festive season and a perfect time to make contact with Stefan. Over cocktails they discussed the books they'd been reading and the bands they'd seen recently. They caught up on the news of their families and friends. They filled each other in on their lives and made each other laugh as though they'd just seen each other yesterday and not a year before. Just when Stefan seemed completely relaxed, Stacey heard herself asking if He was happy without her. Before He could answer she asked if His new life was worth losing her for. She knew she'd hit a nerve but she couldn't stop herself. It was a train wreck. Stefan left the restaurant in tears. Stacey realized that making Him cry like she had done the year before didn't make her feel any better. In her words, "There was obviously some stuff I hadn't dealt with."

Denial

Okay, so this isn't really a moment of weakness. It's more like a deep slump that can linger for a while. You were going along doing fine and all of a sudden you've been walloped in the head with a big red rubber stamp saying DENIAL in bold letters. Unfortunately, this has all the makings of a very public Bittergirl Breakdown.

He calls and asks if He could use the leftover paint sitting in your basement for His new living room. You plan to drop it off right after you've been to the gym. You're lip-synching to the song "I Will Love Again" when you notice a member of His Ultimate Frisbee team approaching the treadmill beside you. You lock eyes with her and she hesitates for a moment before she climbs onto the machine. You shout hello to her. She says something but you can't hear. You turn off your music and ask her to repeat what she just said. She says how sorry she is about what happened. You assure her everything's fine. "I-think-we're-going-over-the-color-scheme-for-His-new-house-tonight-you-should-see-what-we're-thinking-of-for-the-living-room-actually-we're-thinking-of-ordering-in-a-great-new-bedroom-set-for-the-spare-room-and-we're-really-excited-at-what-the-landscape-architect-wants-to-do-with-the-front-lawn-there's-just-so-much-work-to-do-and-thank-God-the-summer-is-coming-because-we'll-be-able-to-put-in-lots-of-time-fixing-up-the-back-deck-you-should-come-over-sometime-and-we-can-have-a-barbe—" She cuts you off. "Actually the team was just there last night. He doesn't have a back deck." "Oh, yeah, well, I mean, we're planning on building one for the summer. You know how stuff like that really bonds you. . . ." She backs down and away from the machine very slowly. She nods tentatively and makes a run for the change room.

This is nasty. Whatever triggered this breakdown must be dealt with IMMEDIATELY. Whether you went off your medication or just checked yourself in to la-la land for the day, the week, the month, we urge you to jump from this train because it is about to become one big, bad, twisted wreck.

Take Jackie. She and Allan had been split up for ages. She'd been stoic, strong, dignified in the face of it all. She still frequented the same old pub He went to and He still lived in the house SHE owned. They still had joint bank accounts because He needed the paperwork in order to stay in the country. She had dated a few guys, was working hard, seemed to be really moving past Allan, when she went to the pub one day with a few bags of groceries. His pals asked where she was headed with all that food. "Home," she sighed. "On Tuesday nights, Allan and I like to just hang out and make dinner and watch TV. It's one of those things we do." His buddies laughed and ordered her a shooter. "Have another one, Jackie," they snickered.

Oh, Jackie. There are so many things wrong with this situation, but the main one is that she went and convinced herself that she and Allan were building a life together again. One day she woke up and decided that since they lived under the same roof, shared financial statements, liked Tuesday night TV, and peed in the same toilet, it must mean something. Well, no, in fact, He just lives in her house because He can live rent-free; if the amount in their bank accounts were reversed He'd be shipped back to Portugal; He likes watching TV on Tuesdays because He can watch whatever He wants AND get a cooked meal to eat while He's at it. Jackie has fabricated a life for them where there is NO LIFE left. Her breakdown just went public and it will take a long time for her to come back from this one.

Sabotage

When we spoke of revenge in Chapter 11, not even your team could have come up with this one. It's not premeditated: A demon completely takes over your body and propels you on a mission to destroy His new relationship. When you finally gain possession of your rational self again, humiliation and embarrassment come hurtling toward you like a car whose brakes were left at the shop. At the time it's happening, though, you're convinced that if you go through with your actions you'll mess up what He has with this other woman and He'll come running back to you. Think again, honey.

The moment Sharina heard the news that Brock was dating one of their oldest friends, Chrissy, she marched over to His house, rang the doorbell, seduced Him on the doorstep, and led Him up to the bedroom. They had wild, crazy sex. Before she left, Sharina made sure to accidentally leave behind one of her one-of-a-kind rhinestone earrings that Chrissy had given her for her birthday last year. There would be no doubt as to who had left it there.

Talia saw Harry sitting with His new squeeze at a local martini bar. She decided it was obvious they weren't having a good time. She sat at the bar, knocked back eight cosmopolitans, then performed a striptease act in front of their table. His new squeeze stormed out of the bar and Harry ran right after her.

The best thing to do after an act of sabotage is block it right out of your memory. Go straight to see an action movie, get drunk with your team, take a canoe trip with your outdoorsy pal. Get as far away from the scenario as possible. By the time you return, hopefully it will seem like a dream, a bad B movie, or a silly rumor that got blown out of proportion. Avoid contact with all parties and isolate yourself from the episode as much as possible.

The Consequences

Although the aftereffects of reunion sex, the middle-of-the-night phone call, or desperate pleas to His family may feel like the worst hangover you've ever had, you cannot dwell on this moment.

You may feel slightly embarrassed because of the brazen hussy you became the night before, you may wince at the thought of His father reading the pathetic birthday card you sent listing all the beautiful qualities that Jacob inherited from Him, you may cringe at the memory of the entire martini bar watching you slide your halter top over your head, but the Bittergirl Breakdown is an important landmark in the journey of a bittergirl.

As Cheryl told us, "We had slept together again. The next day I was lying in my bed, waiting for Connor to call, feeling so low, so down. I was mad at myself because I desperately wanted Him to call and at the same time I just wanted to stop hurting from Him. And then it hit me—I wasn't really hurting from Him. I was hurting from the idea of Him. Nothing could ever come close to the pain I felt when He first left. And if I had handled that, then I could handle this. I got out of bed, threw on some clothes, and went for a walk. He didn't call but at least I wasn't sitting around waiting for the phone to ring."

What Cheryl realized was that once you've gone through The Incident, you can never go back. Can you really imagine feeling any shittier than you did after that? It may seem as though you're on a trajectory back to heartbreak hell, but a Bittergirl Breakdown can give you valuable insight. What it often does is clarify how much farther along you are than you thought. You may feel dismal and pathetic for a little bit, but all those feelings have started to become stale and boring to you.

It may be time to revisit Chapter 4 and rewrite your Contract (see bitteractivities at the end of this chapter). As you do this, we're sure you'll realize that you're not doing so badly after all. You no longer need every item in the Emergency Kit, you don't have to call in sick to work, you realize that the astrology hotline isn't going to help you, and you require only two of your team around you as opposed to six.

The most sobering moment of the Bittergirl Breakdown is actually telling someone about it. As you recount your behavior to your team, your bestbittergirlfriends may nod their heads in recognition of the time they succumbed to a similar fate. They may reprimand you for not seeing straight enough to call in the reinforcements, but they'll understand and see the breakdown for what it is. Would you have acted that way if you'd been surrounded by your team? Not likely. And they know that.

It's important to remember that a Bittergirl Breakdown is short-lived, and it's vital that you keep thinking of it that way. It may feel as though you've taken two steps backward in your bittergirl journey, but this is not a permanent holdup. This is a time to draw on your bittergirl pride. Grab that sense of humor from your bedside table and chalk the experience up to exploring your new personality.

And really think about the breakdown. We mean break it down. Let's be honest. Was the sex really that good? Maybe He's not really such a hotshot in bed. Maybe the way He growls during sex is no longer endearing but outright scary. Maybe that cute little face He makes when He climaxes reminds you of a chihuahua squeezing out a turd. Maybe when He nuzzles His face in the crook of your neck you see that His bald spot is growing exponentially. When you were slipping your bra strap off your shoulder did you notice that He really does have a monobrow?

Maybe the way His mother talks to you isn't sweet; it's condescending. Did you really want to go to Florida AGAIN? To stay in a villa with seventy-year-olds in Speedos and yarmulkas? Didn't holidays with His family truly drive you crazy?

The Bittergirl Breakdown has passed. Hopefully it will never happen again. Every once in a while a bittergirl lets her tiara slip. It's allowed. Just don't let yourself dwell there. Because, honey, the love has died and no amount of reunion sex or phone calls to the family will alter that. You've been allowed your moment of weakness. It's time to give your head a good shake, get back to KUA, and keep going forward with your life. As we said in Chapter 1, this is not about blame. It is, however, about moving on. Simply adjust that tiara, center it firmly on your head, grab your team, and vow to let this become just another notch in your bittergirl belt. Now, if you're in Denial and the breakdown hasn't ended, it's a whole different story. You need to spend some quality time with Chapter 13: "Beyond Bitter."

🍸 bitteractivities

1. Rewrite That Contract   Just to be sure you've put the breakdown behind you, pull out that Contract you signed in Chapter 4. You know the one. It's the piece of paper you used to have glued to your phone, your fridge, your forehead until you thought it was no longer necessary.

Based on certain experiences since then, you may want to revise it or add a few things:

I will not under any circumstances straddle Him and tell Him I'm the star of His personal rodeo.

I will not under any circumstances call Him and sing, "Reunited, and it feels so good."

I will not under any circumstances send His mother a flower arrangement with a card saying, "If only we were still together, I'd still be calling you my mother-in-law. I miss you."

I will not under any circumstances send Him a collage of all our most loving moments and title it "The Love That Will Never Die."

2. Team Breakdown   Make a list of all the breakdowns you've heard about from other people. (Team included!)

thirteen

beyond bitter

DO YOU LOOK AT WEDDING INVITATIONS and think, "Yeah, how long will *they* last?" Do you see a baby boy and say, "How long before he breaks someone's heart?" Your best friend is your vibrator and it has been for eighteen months. Do you refuse a date with the six-foot-tall doctor with the cool blue eyes because you don't want to miss the season finale of *ER*? Are you a trial lawyer who attempts to convince your boss that you can do your job from home? Are the condoms on your bedside table from the Reagan administration? Can you tell us how many times Monica, Chandler, Joey, and Rachel are on TV each day but have no idea what's going on with your own group of friends? When they call to invite you for a night out (if they haven't given up on you already), does your regular list of excuses read something like this: What's the point? We all die alone anyway—I might as well get used to it now. Nothing lasts forever. I've seen it all. There's no such thing as a happy ending. Why would I give some of the best years of my life to someone else? I have nothing more to say.

Darling, you're Beyond Bitter. You may even be housebound. For you there was no recovery in the Bittergirl Breakup Recovery Period. For you it is merely the BP—the Breakup. Period.

It's much easier to stay in on Friday nights and cuddle up with a good book than be out there in the big bad world of heartbreak, disappointment, and shitty relationships. They all end anyway, right? Everyone's taken or gay. Sooner or later everyone gets replaced—either by another woman, a man, a pet, a career. People naturally grow in opposite directions. Nothing is permanent.

I mean, at least you know that when you come home from work everything will be exactly the way you left it. You don't have to do the dishes if you don't feel like it. You can step out of your pajamas in the morning and leave them there to step right back into when you get home. You don't have to worry about whose family you're spending the holidays with. You never have to shave your legs again. You can drink the milk right out of the carton. You don't have to follow Him around cleaning up His messes. You can eat your dinner where God intended you to—in front of the TV with your best friends, *Will & Grace*.

Whether stuck in a time warp, placed firmly in denial, living in a state of constant fear, waffling along in an apathetic state, or laying blame on all members of the opposite sex, the beyondbittergirl is living in a complete vacuum.

If you look up at any high-rise building on a Saturday night, you can safely assume that at least one-eighth of the lit-up windows belong to a beyondbittergirl. Likewise, if you take a drive in the country after dark, scattered across the hillside you will see the twinkle of lights from many a beyondbittergirl abode.

The Bittergirl Institute for Advanced Research on Dumping has delineated four types of beyondbittergirls.

Beyondbittergirls

Time Warp

Hello, Ms. Havisham. Your watch probably reads the exact second, minute, hour that He broke up with you. Your house looks exactly as it did the day He left. You haven't moved a single picture of the two of you. The space in the closet where His clothes used to hang remains empty, as if waiting for His garments to return.

You have used the few belongings He left behind to create a shrine dedicated to Him. The incense is always burning. The flame of a candle flickers constantly over that mahogany-framed photo of Him.

You talk about Him as if He just stepped out for milk. When your colleague Gillian cries on your shoulder you talk about how you and Ron deal with your disagreements. You fail to mention that Ron is happily married to someone else and has three kids. There is no you and Ron.

If you're not careful, your heart will harden to stone. You may think this would be a good alternative, but let's be honest. Why let cobwebs collect in your soul while the rest of the world continues on? You don't have to become the head of the neighborhood social committee, but pushing your shirt hangers over into His half of the closet is a good start.

Do you really want your brother's grandchildren to visit you in the future and ask why their great auntie Evelyn is still wearing a dirty, ratty old wedding gown?

What's the Point?

You might as well be wearing a sign saying STAY BACK 500 FEET. You've got it all figured out. And it all comes down to the same question: "What's the point?"

Why go out? You might actually meet someone. Then you might like Him. He might like you. He might ask you out, kiss you, and then, before you know it, you're dating. You have to get your dog to like Him. You have to introduce Him to your kids, your friends, your family. You have to go through the "Do they like Him, does He like them?" You have to get used to a whole new social circle. You have to meet His family, get to know all their inside jokes. You have to buy another fucking toothbrush for your place and his place. You have to show Him your life. You have to get used to each other in bed—not to mention being bed-ready with shaved legs and a dating body. You have to be able to tell Him what you want. You have to develop a whole new sexual shorthand. You have to attend the first big family celebration. Then you'll have the premonition of another heart-wrenching, soul-destroying breakup, and so you'll have to break up with Him so he doesn't get the satisfaction of breaking up with you first. So what's the point? Honey, you have adopted the *Fatalistic Excuse.*

Why bother? It's the same bar, same conversation, same music, same assholes, same cheesy pickup lines, same "So what do you do for a living, my friend thinks you're cute," same cocktail list, same opening night party hors d'oeuvres, same faces, same fake smiles, same "So good to see you," same air kisses, same feigned interest in your conversation, same propositions. And the same old "Can-I-take-you-home-so-we-can-get-together-and-fall-madly-in-love-and-then-I-can-l eave-you-unexpectedly-because-I-need-another-fix." What's the point? Oh, yes, the *Repetitive Excuse.*

Things are finally back to a life that somewhat resembles normal. You have some kind of schedule back. You couldn't throw that off. It wouldn't be right bringing another person to the dinner table. The kids wouldn't like Him anyway. You can't take your attention away from the children. It's not fair. They need you. You can't introduce your kids to someone who's going to leave you anyway. Then you'd just have to explain why another person left. So what's the point? Nice try, baby, that's the *Childminder Excuse.*

There will ALWAYS be excuses. Admit it: You're afraid. Afraid of getting hurt again. Afraid of making yourself vulnerable. But there will always be scary things in life. Wouldn't it be boring otherwise? Can you imagine knowing how each day is going to play out for the rest of your life? BORING! Well, at the rate you're going, not much is going to change. Remember when you were learning to ride a bike? You fell off. It hurt. You got back on. You fell off again. Cried a little, then got back on. You didn't sit on the sidewalk saying there's no point in ever getting on anything with two wheels because it will only end up in pain and agony, did you? Take a lesson from yourself. Get back on the bike. It doesn't mean you have to stay on it for very long. But at least take it for a test ride.

Apathy Girl

You reject invitations to functions that might be couples-heavy. When you book your vacation you use the "Going Solo" travel company. You stress to the travel agent that you will ride a bicycle 140 miles rather than sit on a bus tour full of vacationing families.

You adamantly refuse to attend dinner parties where you'll be paired up with someone to make the numbers even. You avoid anything that celebrates love: weddings, baby showers, engagement celebrations, anniversary parties. You recoil at the thought of a blind date. You have no patience for the idea of flowers and romance; wine-and-dine is an individual activity for you. Your relationship history says it all, you argue. There's no way you'll invest the time even thinking about the possibility of any emotional attachment to a person of the opposite sex.

Relationship Apathy can hit the best of the bittergirls, honey. Too many dumpings, too much disappointment, too many bad blind dates. It can leave a stale taste in many a bittergirl's mouth and an expired best-before date on her forehead.

Even if you opened your heart to being in a room with single men or, heaven forbid, entertained the notion of dating again, we bittergirls know there's not a hope in hell for even the Adonises of the world. You see, Apathy Girl lives way up high in her hundred-foot tower of impenetrable steel. If, and that's a big IF, she ever dates again, He will have to be perfect. He'll have to make up for every disappointment she's ever had and will have to possess every quality that Apathy Girl desires. He must be a Cancer, He must have sandy brown hair, He must wear the right shoes, He must be between five-ten and five-eleven-and-a-half, He must have been to the Galápagos, He must like Siamese cats, He must have read Dostoevsky, He must be vegan, He must do his own taxes, He must tie his shoelaces in the over-under method, He must, He must, He must, He must. . . .

Ah, Apathy Girl, when the perfect man comes along, we'll be sure to clone Him and let you know. Until then, YOU HAVE TO LIVE IN REALITY. Try walking down the steps of your tower and slipping into the world again. Let yourself chuckle at all the imperfections that make life so grand. There is no perfect man and, ahem, surprise, surprise, you might not be so perfect yourself. So, dust off the Manolos, sass yourself up, and venture to a party that might just end up in even pairings. We're not asking you to prostitute yourself in your social circle, but you might just find yourself having some interesting conversations and maybe even flirting a little while you're at it. Don't you remember when flirting was fun? Why not take a stab at it again and see how it feels. You still get to take yourself home at the end of the night, and you'll still be in control of your own feelings. And hey, you just might have a little bit of good, clean fun.

More than a year after her last breakup, Christiana, a now re-formed beyondbittergirl, flatly refused to accept any invitations to functions with couples. This greatly limited her options, and as her friends grew tired of her adolescent behavior, they simply stopped inviting her to things. Three years later, Christiana was in a healthy, happy relationship and engaged to be married. When she went to send out the invitations to her couples shower she realized she had ostracized some of the most important people in her life by being beyond bitter. Dear bittergirl, don't let this happen to you.

Bitter Woman

Whoa, there's no doubt that you're bitter. Everywhere you go you make that very clear. Beware any man who crosses your path. If he's not careful he'll be inundated by the backlog of hate that has accumulated in your heart. And once you've vented on this poor fellow, your pit of disenchantment will refill itself until your next encounter with an unwitting member of the male species.

You've formed a group of like-minded women that meets on a monthly basis. You latch on to anyone who has a painful story and ensnare her in your clutches. You thrive on the mutual misery you've all endured. Blame is the name of the game. You recite pure hate poetry and share dirty jokes at the expense of your exes and their new flames. You thrive on acidic anecdotes and take no accountability for the relationship breakdown. You will never ever love a man again.

Well, you may never love a man again, but that's not actually the problem here. Whether you realize it or not, you may be shutting yourself off from a lot more than the possibility of love. Sooner or later people get sick of being around so much anger and negativity. Bitter Woman is Angry Girl who never got over it. We're here to say, get over it. We're not saying you should feel sorry for Him, that you need to forgive Him, or even that you think of Him at all; we're saying that you can't label every male in the human race as being just like Him.

A bittergirl may harbor resentment toward the perpetrator of her breakup, but she eventually recognizes that He's the one who really missed out. A bittergirl doesn't need another man to fill her life, but she's sassy and confident and knows that one day she might just *choose* to invite someone in.

Arlene was devastated after the dissolution of her marriage. Matters were only made worse when He made public His new relationship with their real estate broker. Arlene sealed her heart for good and vowed never to be hurt again. Instead of just hating Him, she channeled all her energy into hating every member of the opposite sex. She sent man-hating joke e-mails and stories to her entire female address book. It was funny at first, but after a while her friends began blocking her e-mail address and slowly stopped returning her calls. Her daughters finally had to give her an ultimatum. Smarten up or lose us as friends too.

movies with bitter women

Fatal Attraction

The Hand That Rocks the Cradle

Single White Female

Disclosure

Gone With the Wind

Chicago

Dangerous Liaisons

The War of the Roses

The bittergirls were on public transit the other day (the limo was in the shop) and an older woman climbed on and found herself a seat. Looking up, she caught the eye of an attractive young man and decided that he was, for whatever reason, flirting with her. She started to talk to him, chatting at first in that slightly inappropriate, not-in-public kind of way, which eventually got louder and louder until it bloomed into a full-blown harangue that took in the entire bus. She had apparently decided to have it out with him on behalf of herself and all her failed romances and the entire female sex.

💋 bittergirlspeak

This is a bitter woman. That screaming banshee of a bus passenger is a non-bittergirl, the non-bittergirl that some of us in our heart of hearts fear we someday could become, left to our own devices and the unfairness of love. Not that she doesn't have the right to express her opinion, and certainly she seemed to have had more than her fair share of bad relationship karma, but none of us wants to be of a certain age and reduced to venting our frustration to the bleary-eyed rush-hour passengers of the downtown express.

What's a Beyondbittergirl to Do?

We've said it before but never has it been truer than now: Every breakup has its shelf life. Eventually the story grows tired and old. Friends will run out of patience and even telemarketers will start hanging up on you.

And if you still insist on defining yourself by your breakup, you're simply giving other people permission to do the same. Although it might be hard for a beyondbittergirl to believe, your breakup may actually be small potatoes to someone who's lost their job and has to support the family or is caring for a terminally ill loved one. Perspective is everything. Believe us, worse things could happen.

Spend an afternoon in the waiting room of the E.R. to give yourself a different point of view. Volunteer at a local AIDS hospice or spend a few hours with a baby and you might learn a few things.

You could stay filled with hate, anger, sadness, blame, humiliation, and fear, or you could make a choice to let it all go. Think how much lighter it will feel.

All this energy you're putting into avoiding life, into staying isolated from all social interaction, into making excuses, or into being angry could be put toward building a new home for yourself, changing your career, helping other people, forging new and lasting friendships, cultivating hobbies, and opening up whole new worlds for yourself.

Let us repeat: *Every breakup has its shelf life.*

beyondbittergirls

Courtney Love

Liza Minnelli

Marlene Dietrich

Judy Garland

Sandra Bernhardt

Ms. Havisham

Queen Elizabeth I

Lorena Bobbitt

Amy Fisher

WARNING: The following stories contain sad and pathetic behavior. They may not be appropriate for all readers.

When Sean dumped Martina, she was a mess for a year. One year turned into two, which turned into four, which turned into seven. In those years, Martina's behavior became more and more extreme. Once lovely and outgoing with a quick wit and great laugh, Martina's conversations now began with "Did you hear the latest about Sean?" Her formerly sympathetic friends became fed up with her one-track mind as they dealt with the ups and downs of their own lives. When Martina began spreading damaging rumors about Sean's professional life, He finally did what He'd hoped He could avoid and had a restraining order put out against her. In an attempt to explain herself, she defied the order and was arrested. So what does she have to show for those seven years of her life? A police record.

Sheila was in such a slump after Dominic dumped her that her doctor prescribed antidepressants. The medication began working but the side effects caused Sheila to gain weight. She became so embarrassed by the way she looked that she stopped going out and cut herself off from a lot of her friends. She sank farther into a depression and the doctor upped her dosage. Her job performance suffered and she was forced to take a compassionate leave of absence. This meant that Sheila was now cut off from her work friends too. She had little contact with the outside world and for a long period of time remained completely HOUSEBOUND. After her company urged her to take advantage of her employee services help benefits, she had a personal life coach come to her apartment. The coach asked her to draw a timeline of the events that led up to that moment and it looked like this:

Heartbreak → depressed → antidepressants → weight gain → embarrassment in public → cut off from friends → more depressed → more drugs → leave of absence from work → further isolation → HOUSEBOUND.

The personal life coach said, "And why? All because some asshole dumped you?"

Sheila looked at the timeline and realized how ridiculous it seemed. With help from the life coach and a lot of bittergirl determination, she slowly reversed the timeline until the point that Dominic dumped her. Then she rewrote her timeline for the next year. Sheila is now living happily with her Wheaton terrier and a fantastic roommate. She's also training to become a life coach. Now that is the true bittergirl way.

If you're reading this in horror and saying to yourself, "OhmyGodamIreallythatbitter?" never fear, beyondbittergirl, we're still here. We are announcing a CALL TO ACTION. The alarm bells are ringing and the bittergirl emergency hotline is buzzing. It's time to start fresh! Because Beyond Bitter turns into beyond boring. When you're Beyond Bitter, it's like staying at a party too long. Deep down you know you should leave but for some reason you just don't. The hostess is twiddling her thumbs, wondering if you have anywhere to go. Well, the good news in this situation is that you're both the hostess and the lingering party guest. So, kick yourself out and see where you end up. We guarantee it'll be a better place.

Go back to Chapters 3 and 4, rebuild your team if you have to, then place that tiara firmly on your head and return on the bittergirl journey. You see, the bittergirls know from experience that if you can bring yourself to visualize the most fabulous life imaginable for yourself, eventually you'll find a way to live that life. But first you have to make the choice to return from the land of Beyond Bitter and rejoin the human race. Getting back out there doesn't mean diving into the dating pool. It doesn't require a man. In fact, it doesn't require anything—it just means living a life.

✑ bitteractivities

1. Celebration Creation   Find something to celebrate. It can be as random or significant as you'd like. Invite all your friends (yes, both male and female) and ask them to join in the festivities. Go whole hog. Be daring, be cheeky, be creative.

Here's a smart idea to get your creative juices flowing: Ilana decided to celebrate the end of the Year of the Goat. She had a goat piñata and everyone at the party had to whack the piñata and shout out the thing they most wanted to relinquish from the previous year. She'd asked her guests to bring a wish for the new year, and over a glass of champagne everyone read their wish and raised a toast to the future. Now that's a true bittergirl celebration. Whack the shit out of the past and drink to the future.

2. Box Him Up   If you're still holding on to Him and have ANY of His stuff left in your immediate vicinity, gather it up. This list might include things that just remind you of Him—big or small. And yes, that goes for anything from key rings to shoelaces to cotton sheets. Put them in a box and consign the box to storage: in a basement, attic, or far corner of a deep closet. Better yet, take it all to the nearest Goodwill and get rid of it.

fourteen
bittergirl bonding

OKAY, DARLING. You're out in the world, you're doing things, you're living a life again.

So we have a suggestion. How's about a little celebration of you and all you've achieved so far? Did you make it to the subway station without a breakdown today? When He e-mailed looking for the extension cord He left behind, did you leave it with your doorman? When He called asking about that insurance policy, did you not call Him back for three days because you really were too busy? Good for you! That's an achievement in our books, and we think you need to lift a frosty glass to that.

Bittergirl bonding is the most entertaining part of the BBRP. This is a time for creating your own rituals, establishing new ceremonies, and making new anniversaries for yourself. You get to celebrate your fabulousness, along with the fabulousness of your team and your very bestbittergirlfriends. Fashion your own fantastic party nights, make a fuss over yourselves, and honor your full, extraordinary lives.

Bittergirl bonding is like a book club, a girls' poker night, a gourmet dinner club, a curling cluster, and a running group all rolled into one. It can be any or all of these things and much, much more. Your wish is your command. Your pleasure is whatever you want it to be. How fantastic is that? Any whim you desire? Create it, fulfill it, and laugh out loud as you revel in the fact that the snapshot you put in your memory bank way back in Chapter 1 is almost fully developed.

If you haven't yet, this is the perfect time to reclaim your space or warm your new house. Invite your bestbittergirlfriends and have a *bittergirls' night in.* This achieves several goals in one fell swoop. You are in control. It takes place on your turf. And it will force you to shape up that turf a bit. Tidy up some of those empty pizza boxes and scrape a layer of grime off the bathroom sink.

Let's be clear: You don't have to kill yourself in a Martha Stewart frenzy here. Once again, it's all about KUA, and you can keep them up without causing yourself undue stress.

Grab some candles. They're a bittergirl's best friend. Who can see the dust bunnies when the lights are low? Pull the shower curtain. In a few days you'll feel like scrubbing that tub, but who's going to take a bath here tonight? No one, that's who.

Head to the nearest dollar store and pick up a whole bunch of brightly colored flip-flops. Your girlfriends will love having their own pair to slip into and you don't have to worry about scrubbing the hardwood floors clean.

Dirty dishes? In the dishwasher. Dirty laundry? In the closets or under the bed. Closets are there for a reason, so shove whatever you need into them and close the door.

Tidy up the visible mess and you'll feel better about yourself, but leave the major housecleaning for when you're feeling up to it. If anyone's going to criticize the state of your carpet they are not the bittergirlfriends you want in your house tonight. One of our bestbittergirlfriends once said that if anyone mentions the dust on the floors, your unwashed hair, or the lukewarm hors d'oeuvres, turn up the heat, pour them a double, and scratch them off the guest list for next time.

Now, what's on the menu?

Like we say about cleaning the house, this evening is all about you and celebrating your life, not about stressing over the particulars. You can order in, you can buy takeout. But if you feel like cooking, pick something that takes as little effort as humanly possible.

The bittergirls say: Grazing is Good. One of the best meals you can have with your friends is a chilled bottle of wine and a selection of dips, pita, veggies, and any finger foods you feel like. If you feel like picking up some sushi and serving it next to hummus and taramasalata, you go for it. Sitting around the table and eating food with your fingers with your best friends and a good wine is a fine way to get all the major food groups into your system. Put out some napkins and plates and have a lovely bittergirlnightin.

Here are a couple of five-minute-prep meals, one chicken and one pasta—buy some lovely bread and a bag of salad and some dressing and you have a meal any bittergirl can be proud of without breaking a sweat (and you can enjoy your conversation with your BBGFs instead of spending the evening sweating in the kitchen trying to roll some damn chicken breasts around kiwi and pine nuts and gorgonzola). Believe us, these recipes have been tested in our bittergirl kitchen under the most trying of circumstances: One heartbroken bittergirl tucked into the cooking sherry before she started any cooking, and another's eyes were so swollen from crying that she put four tablespoons of chilies into a recipe that called for a quarter of a teaspoon!

A Couple of Easy Bittergirl Recipes

Moira's Chicken

Moira first made this dish when the man was gone, the kids were hungry, the alcoholic mother-in-law was coming over to visit, and she absolutely HAD to pull herself together. It's been a staple ever since in her kitchen and ours. Gussy it up with some olives and capers and julienned red pepper instead of the veggies, and pour a slurp of white wine in with the chicken broth—you can do anything with it and it still tastes good.

Throw one cut-up chicken or bag of chicken pieces into a baking dish—use as much or as little chicken as you need to feed your fabulous bestbittergirlfriends.

Pour one cup of chicken stock over the chicken. Chop a carrot or two, a stalk of celery (with the greenery), and a parsnip. (This is all about what's easiest: Don't have a carrot? Chop some red or green pepper. No celery? Shred a leaf of lettuce or use the carrot-top greenery. No parsnip? A couple of mushrooms, an onion, whatever else is handy will do. It's just adding flavor anyway.)

Sprinkle on top a handful of dried herb mix: Herbes de Provence works best but you can use an Italian mix or experiment with any combo of your own. Add a splash of white wine, pour yourself a glass, and relax. Cover the dish with foil and cook at 350 degrees for 45 minutes, then remove foil and cook for another 15 minutes or until the chicken is a little crispy on top. Serve with rice or pasta or potatoes, maybe some beans and a salad and bread. See? So so so simple.

Sweet Pepper Pasta

Ling-ling is a vegan, so she adapted this recipe from Joie Warner's *All the Best Pasta Sauces* when she was tired of eating cold bagels with soy cheese and was weeping into her pasta pot.

The most difficult thing you have to do in this recipe is pit and chop 20 Greek olives. So do that first and put them aside in a bowl with ⅓ cup of capers and a handful of chopped fresh parsley. Then chop 1 red, 1 yellow, and 1 orange pepper, 1 red onion, and 4 cloves of garlic. Boil some water and cook enough penne for four to six people.

While the pasta's cooking, throw the peppers and onion and garlic in a skillet with ⅓ cup of oil and cook and stir for 10 minutes. Add ½ cup of pine nuts and cook for another 5 minutes or until they go golden. Sprinkle in a tablespoon of dried basil. Stir, then add the olives and peppers, onions, and parsley, and some salt and pepper.

Toss with the drained pasta (it should have been done a few minutes ago), throw it all in a big serving bowl, and put it out on the table with bread and salad and some fresh parmesan for the nonvegans. Easy peasy.

Dessert? There's nothing, we repeat nothing, as easy and tasty as dessert that takes no effort. One of our bittergirls makes wonderful cakes, but what with the fabulous bakeries in your town and Sara Lee in every grocery store the world over, there's no excuse for stress over dessert. Buy some fruit. Cut it up. Put out a couple of your favorite flavors of store-bought gelato and a plate of delicious brownies or blondies. Open another bottle of wine. Life is good.

Drinks, Anyone?

Now, it has come to the bittergirls' attention that there are some poor souls out there in the world who don't know how to make a martini. For shame. How did that happen? Next thing we know you'll be telling us your mother didn't give you an oyster knife and a champagne recorker when you moved away from home.

We sigh for the good old days of *The Thin Man* when Nick and Nora Charles shook up a shaker at the drop of a hat.

Basic Bone-Dry Bittergirl Martini

You'll need ice, good-quality gin, and a little dry vermouth (we've always been partial to Noilly Prat). Some good stuffed olives or a twist of lemon if you prefer for garnish. Take your martini shaker and pour a capful of dry vermouth into it, then POUR IT OUT. Put several ice cubes into the shaker and a couple of ounces of gin per person. Put on the lid and shake it up, baby. Strain your martinis into some nice glasses. Garnish to your heart's delight.

No shaker? Or maybe you live by the "stirred, never shaken—bruises the gin" rule. Make up a pitcher of martinis and stir carefully—hold the ice if you do. Or to make them glass by glass, do like the catering bartenders do and pour a teeny bit of dry vermouth into a glass, swirl it around to coat the glass, then POUR IT OUT. Add the gin. For a truly dry martini, hold the vermouth altogether and add a drop of Scotch to the bottom of your glass. Don't forget the olives!

Variations

Make mine a vodka martini! Same recipe, only use a good (cold) vodka.

Dirty Martini: Add to your basic martini a little of the lovely liquid the olives have been floating in before you shake it up. Yummy—a little fiber with your martini. It's your Dirty Little Secret.

Classic Cosmo: Made with 2 ounces vodka, 1 ounce Cointreau, ½ ounce lime juice, and 1 splash cranberry juice. Throw them in the shaker, honey! And strain it. It's a girly favorite, so let's call this one **The Coward**.

Lemon Martini: Take 1½ jiggers vodka, ½ ounce triple sec, ½ ounce Amaretto, and a small squeeze of 1 lemon wedge, and shake them in your invaluable shaker with ice. Squeeze what's left of the wedge into a martini glass and then pour the mixture into the glass. Garnish with a lemon twist. We like to call this little number **The Fucker Pucker**.

Crantini, or as we like to call it, The Mountie: Mix 1½ ounces vodka, ½ ounce triple sec, ½ ounce vermouth, 4 ounces cranberry juice, and some ice cubes in a martini shaker. Shake and strain into a martini glass and garnish with a cranberry or two. (Soak the cranberries in vodka first if you're feeling fancy.)

Chocolate Martini: 1 part white crème de cacao and 1 part vodka. Shake ingredients with ice, then strain into a shot glass. White and creamy, just like . . . hello, **Trigger**.

Manhattan: One bittergirl's dad taught her at an early age to mix up a good Manhattan. 2 parts rye whiskey, one part sweet vermouth, and a dash of bitters. Shake with ice and strain into a glass. Maybe you'll find **MIA** in Manhattan.

Kamikaze, or as we like to call it, Man Solo: 1⅓ ounces vodka, 1 ounce triple sec, 1 ounce lime juice. Serve as a classic shooter or stir all the ingredients with ice; strain into a chilled tumbler filled with ice, and garnish with a lime twist.

Or, here's a pitcher of shooters you can mix up for your BBGFs and name for yourselves: Mix 3 ounces peach schnapps,

1½ ounces gin, 1½ ounces coconut rum, 1½ ounces vodka, and a mixture that's ⅓ pineapple juice, ⅓ orange juice, and ⅓ cranberry juice in a pitcher full of ice. Stir well and serve.

Use your imagination! Or buy a bartender's bible and mix away—or look up your favorite drink combos on the Internet. Make your favorite drink and give it your favorite nickname. Invite your bestbittergirlfriends to christen their own drinks. Write them down and immortalize them—then you can get your local bartender to mix them up for you when you're out for a night on the town. And maybe someday you'll have the satisfaction of seeing your ex sit down at a bar somewhere and order His very own Fucker Pucker.

bittergirl shot faves

No More Sex on the Beach

I Always Faked My Orgasm

I Hated Giving You a Blow Job

Bitterpartyactivities

What's your game plan for the evening? Well that depends on where you are in your BBRP.

If you are still anti-Him, then here's where you delve into the exercises we've given you and turn them into an event.

Darts Night

Find that photo of Him and tack it to the dart board. Or would you prefer to play pin the tail on the donkey? He's the ass. . . .

Burning Him in Effigy

There's nothing quite as purifying as fire. We've talked about the bittergirls who've burned that special something; many of us have enjoyed the psychic cleansing of a group hug by the Hibachi when what's fueling that BBQ is the detritus left behind by Him. So go to town, bittergirl.

Rainstick

Pass the rainstick and tell your stories. It's cathartic to share and comforting to know that the women sitting around you can tell their stories with hindsight and humor. Don't have a rainstick? Use anything else phallic in the house: a rolling pin, a pestle, your large round hairbrush . . . a baseball bat? Vibrator? Let your imagination guide you—the dirtier the better.

Drinking Game

Come on, we don't have to help you with this one! You were the one who invented the dorm-room favorite "Sound of Music Jell-O Shots." Every time you refer to Him you have to take a slug of that lovely champers Janine brought. Every time you think about Him you have to pour everyone a shot of crème de menthe. Open the window and shout "I am getting over Him!" and then you all down your minty-fresh shots together. Or something like that—you get the idea. (Extend this into your everyday life and resolve to throw out a pair of shoes every time you start to dial His number—that'll break the habit fast.)

A Little Help from Your Friends

It's usually Reasonable Girl who ends up in a situation like this: He phones and asks for all the pictures He's in from their mutual photo album. He wants them back—He wants to start His own collection of memories, without Reasonable. She reasonably says okay because, after all, she didn't want them anymore anyway. . . . Bittergirls, she needs her bestbittergirlfriends! To sit on the floor with Reasonable Girl and pull those photos out, to rewrite their history and put back together her photo album and her life.

For anything like this—any request from Him that's just too hard for your delicate soul to take at this moment—turn it into a celebration of your life yet to come with your bestbittergirlfriends, because that's what they're here for.

Which brings us to our next kind of bittergirlnightin: *a celebration of you.*

The Today I's

This also involves your dirty little rainstick and some quality bonding. Pass the phallic symbol and tell us what you've achieved today.

Today I found the nape of another man's neck sexy.
Today I woke up before my alarm clock.
Today I realized that I don't want to understand football.
Today I bought my own garlic press.
Today I shaved my legs.
Today I took Him off my speed dial.
Today I didn't drive past His house once!
Today I read only *my* horoscope.

This can also morph into a drinking game—can't think of today's achievement? Have a drink, bittergirl.

Clothing Swap

Clean out your cupboards and purge yourself of Him. Did He love you in cute little twin sets? Bundle them up—Sarah will look fantastic in them when she wears the cardigan over her bustier and the shell under her frayed overalls. And she never wears that turquoise halter now that she's pregnant and you've always loved it. . . . A cheap way to reinvigorate your wardrobe, get together with the BBGFs, and clear out the remaining cobwebs of your old life with Him.

Do-It-Yourself

Invite a Home Renovation guy to come in and give a workshop on how to build things. Tell him there's twenty bucks extra in it if he'll take his shirt off. Choose a project and get your hands dirty. Building stuff is a great metaphor for you right now. And we all know how good it feels to give something a good screw. Think about how much better Denial Girl from Chapter 12 would have felt if she was able to tell His Ultimate Frisbee teammate on the Stairmaster that she was doing fine and was spending the month focusing on building her very own deck at her very own house.

Garage Sale

Maybe not in your home, but another fabulous celebration you can have with your BBGFs. Make yourself some extra cash off those self-help books you bought and don't need anymore, or that lava lamp He insisted on having in the living room. If you are eager for good karma, donate your earnings to the local women's shelter.

Sex Toys Saleabration

Face it, you're going to use them. You lost your other half, not your libido. And you'll get a chance to see what you've been missing since you've been wrapped up in monogamy. Laugh? You don't know laughter till you've been in a room with eight of your nearest and dearest, several bottles of wine, and a saleswoman who looks like she stepped out of a 1960s Sears catalog demonstrating something large, pink, and battery operated called The Twizzler. Bring in "the lady who teaches you to strip for fun." (And no, we don't mean Talia from Chapter 12.) How can you take yourself seriously as four of you pretend to strip for Bob, the blow-up doll? Or as you watch Mei, your perennially pregnant friend, try to shimmy her shoulders forward only to get stopped short by her belly? And who knows, maybe it's a skill that could come in handy someday in the future.

You Don't Have to Put Out the Red Light

Post-Breakup Roxanne was sick of spending holidays alone. When her birthday rolled around she decided to start a bittergirl bonding tradition. She invited all her bestbittergirlfriends, her team, away for a girls' weekend of R&R. They spent the whole time playing board games, eating, laughing, drinking, napping, reading, going for walks, telling stories, doing WHATEVER THEY WANTED TO DO. This was ten years ago. A few are single, a few are married, and a few more have kids, but every November this group of women congregates for a weekend to celebrate Roxanne's fabulousness with unstructured time together.

"My Name's on the Guest List"

In the movies when the main character gets dumped, she's usually surrounded by a group of glamorous single friends with posh accents, cool jobs, and names like Kip, Saffy, and Arabella. In reality, when *you* get dumped, you may be surrounded by friends, but Muriel listens to your sobs between "No Zoe, don't eat the kitty litter," "Honey I don't know where your car keys are," and "Can you hold on? I have to verify this policy claim."

You may not have the stylish big-city gay friend with the droll quips, but your pal Paul the plumber might just know the exact right thing to say at the right moment in his own awkward way. Instead of being there for you 24/7, you may have to book your team three weeks in advance between their quarterly reports and kids' basketball tournaments. You may not get them solo as often as you'd like and you may find yourself sharing them with their other half. So your evenings of bittergirl bonding may become coed from time to time or involve three bedtime stories and two glasses of juice.

There are positives to this: Your bestbittergirlfriend's husband may just end up becoming a bestbittergirlfriend too; you might gain a perspective on things that hadn't previously occurred to you; and sometimes it does make a difference when somebody other than your best friend tells you that you're doing well and looking fantastic. And while you may not relish the thought of pedicures and Dom Perignon with half her hubby's soccer team, you may be surprised at how pleasant drinks after their game, pizza after the play, or cocktails after the concert can be in mixed company. Remember the Anti-Bittergirl who excluded you because you weren't half of a couple anymore? Well, don't you exclude your BBGFs just because they're part of a couple too.

Instead of dismissing Harvey's obsession with Australian-rules rugby, Shauna started watching it with him and Jennifer and learned some of the finer points while hanging out with her pals. And sports made small talk so easy! Shauna found that once you understand a sport, you can chat with anyone over the water cooler or the lunch counter or the canapé tray, and she developed a much better relationship with her boss when she discovered he was a closet rugby freak. The firm is announcing her promotion next Thursday.

The Road Less Traveled

Two disillusioned bittergirls felt trapped in their social circle because they kept running into their respective Hims. It was summertime and they realized they were just sitting around waiting for things to happen. So they bonded in true bittergirl fashion, rented a car, and packed it up with camping gear and other luxuries. They took the lead from Thelma and Louise and set off on a road trip: destination unknown. They didn't take a map, they just followed their instincts.

They ended up having hilarious adventures, meeting wonderful people whom they're now great friends with, and most of all, they did it in style. Instead of sleeping bags, they took their down comforters and their fluffy pillows. They cooked gourmet meals like shrimp alfredo with snow peas on spinach fettuccine over the Coleman stove. They drank red wine under the stars out of their faux crystal (plastic) goblets as they listened to *Madame Butterfly* on their portable radio.

And driving home in the red convertible they'd rented for the weekend, they pulled off their tops and reveled in their newfound bittergirl freedom. After all, who needs tan lines? This is now their summer ritual, and they can be seen every July driving the back roads topless, traveling wherever their instincts take them.

♉ bitteractivities

1. Eat and Drink Him Up   In line with the bittergirl bonding festivities, plan a menu from the predinner drinks and appetizers right down to the after-dessert liqueurs. Creatively name each drink and food item as per your bittergirl journey, making sure to finish off your night with a triumphant, celebratory drink.

Some Sassy Suggestion Samplers
Dastardly Dumplings or Tear-Stained Tatziki, Restaurant Breakup Risotto, Bittergirl Beef Tenderloin, Got Drunk and Fucked His Best Friend Brian Burgers, Begged Him to Come Back Borscht, Slapped His Face Foie Gras, Didn't Cry on Our Anniversary Cake. And to cap the night off, a round of the Fuck You Frangelico.

2. Go Team!   Pick a day of the year and declare it the *International Day of Your BBGFs*. Celebrate in true bittergirl style. Feel free to use any of the bonding activities described in this chapter or gather your team around you and honor at least one trait of each team member à la Dorothy in *The Wizard of Oz*. "And to my Scout for her sense of humor and for finding out He was invited to Angus's party and letting me know in time." Or, you could offer to babysit for a mom, or help another paint her deck. It's a thanks for the memories, in that wiping-the-puke-off-your-face-before-letting-you-head-back-to-the-party-in-the-early-BBRP-days kind of way.

fifteen

that magic moment

So it's been a while. Or maybe it hasn't. Maybe you have amazing recuperative powers and realized fairly quickly what kind of a cad you were dealing with. Maybe not. Maybe it took time—maybe seasons have passed or you've rung in more than one New Year without Him. Maybe you cried your heart out and then came to realize that you didn't want to buy any more tissues. Or maybe you took a long hard look at yourself in the mirror and realized that you were worth more than He thought you were.

The point is, you're over Him.

That magic moment sometimes happens in a blinding flash. Other times it can happen without your even noticing. Our three charter bittergirls were having lunch one day in a restaurant when one noticed that this was the place He took her on their first date. Then one of the others realized that she'd been dumped at this very table. Whatever. They chuckled, poured another glass of wine, and toasted their collective experiences in life.

You will get over Him, we've said throughout this book, and now look! You are. Good for you. You've made it through the BBRP. As

Winston Churchill so aptly put it, "It's time to place a veil over the horrors of the past." Yes, honey, it's that time.

That snapshot that we asked you to imagine back in Chapter 1—do you remember what it looked like? We asked you to visualize the most fabulous life you could possibly imagine. If we asked you to picture that life now, what would it include? You might find it slightly different. You might have achieved some or all of it. You're focusing on you now; the players may be different, the scenery might have changed, but there you are in all your fabulousness and nowhere to go but up.

It's never easy mending a broken heart. A wise woman once said that you never get over some things—you just get used to them. They're always there in your memory, but time mends and eventually even the worst of wounds heal.

And no matter what the process, no matter how little or how long it took, there's a crystalline moment of clarity when you know that this is it and you're really through with Him. It could be simple and comparative: You don't cry when Neil Diamond comes on the oldies radio station anymore. Or complicated: You were at a fundraiser for the charity He's always worked for and you a) didn't realize He might be there; b) didn't care that He was there once you saw Him; and c) didn't have time to talk to your pal when she phoned you the next day to tell you that He disappeared into the bar and drank Himself silly after seeing you, repeating over and over "I am an idiot, what was I thinking" as He whacked His furrowed forehead with His clenched fist. Nope, none of it fazed you.

Well congratulations, honey. You are now officially a full-fledged bittergirl. That's right, you're a bittergirl, not a Bitter Woman. It has nothing to do with age and everything to do with attitude. A Bitter Woman never learned to take the sadness and channel it somewhere worthwhile, to turn the dross into gold, if you will. A Bitter Woman is entrenched in her bitterness, drowning in a sea of unhappiness, unable to come up for air except to shout at those around her. A bittergirl knows how to order a martini, to call up her bestbittergirlfriends, and to get it all out of her system. A bittergirl knows what she's worth, and that her worth is priceless.

bittergirls share their "I knew I was over him" moments

"We slept together after a mutual friend's wedding. The next morning I woke up to find Him sprawled across the bed wearing nothing but a pair of white sports socks."

"He had me paged out of a meeting to see if I could bail Him out of jail."

"He told me in front of our friends, 'No, let's not take a taxi—let's walk—you could use the exercise.' "

"My mother saw Him at the beach. He was wearing a red Speedo."

"When He came to pick up His stuff He asked if a 'pickle wash' was out of the question."

"I finally got tired of Him using my bank card to buy worms and smokes."

"He was a couples therapist but I realized He had commitment issues."

"He said He left me because He needed to be alone. Yeah, alone with our former babysitter."

"He moved in with His mother."

"I saw Him at our son's school play and caught myself wondering if little Joey would inherit His jowls."

"I finally got offered that dream job and He wasn't the first person I thought of calling."

". . . and tonight I'm wearing my engagement ring that I ended up paying for. . . ."

Now that the relationship is over and you're Over Him, you can look back on it with some objectivity. It's not as painful to think about it anymore, so now it becomes less about what you've lost and more about what you're taking with you. Maybe it's as simple as a memory of a trip you took together. Now when you look at the pictures in your photo album you can remember how great the retsina was instead of thinking, "I can never go back to Greece again—that's where He first told me He loved me." You didn't know how to kayak before you met Him—now you're the champion women's paddler at the Harborside Kayaking Society. He was a cynic and you always felt like you'd won the lottery when He finally laughed at your jokes—so open mic night at the local comedy club wasn't such a big deal after your breakup. His inability to take risks drove you so crazy that it prompted you to take bigger ones—and because you're innately cautious and sensible, they keep paying off. So instead of "I lost Him," you can think in positives about what you've gained.

If you totally negate everything in the relationship, then you've totally negated yourself. If He really was such a moron, why the hell were you with Him for five years? He may not have turned out to be your knight in shining armor, but there was valuable life experience in that relationship somewhere. Marie had a miserable long-term breakup with The Coward, but in her quest to keep Him happy she developed the skills in her career that enabled her, by the time He finally left, to move to the top of her profession. Stephanie always thought she was happy in her nine-year relationship, until the last six months when The Mountie went crazy and dumped her. But once

He left she realized she had sublimated her own life choices, and it became very clear to her what she had to do to move ahead the way she'd really always wanted to. And she did.

At the end of the day, what did you walk away with? Now that you're over Him, now that you're past Relationship Mythology, you can give yourself permission to remember the good and the bad in the relationship and maybe learn a few things about yourself. You learned how to finance a mortgage with Him, you created two beautiful children together, you got through your thirties together.

Think about everything you've learned in the last while. You know you can recover from heartache and emerge stronger and better than ever before. You know who your friends are. You know what you're capable of and you know you chose not to do some of the more heinous things you could have done to wreak revenge.

You've survived at work. You've walked into social situations that you may not have enjoyed, but you did it. You got out there, you celebrated yourself, you celebrated your friendships. You've learned the power of the fabulous worldwide sisterhood. Honey, does it get any better than this? We don't think so.

And in the end, you've learned that you're a capable, competent, successful woman. You can do this. Others have. And now you know that you can too.

Remember in third grade when your very bestest friend moved across the country? You swore undying friendship and devotion. For months after, recess felt like purgatory, lunch hour an eternity. But when she came back for a visit during summer vacation something was different. Sure you were thrilled to see her, but the old schoolyard games just weren't as much fun. She didn't know about the time Mr. Chase the gym teacher dropped Elizabeth's peanut butter sandwich and how you all laughed. She didn't seem to care. Was she always this bossy? She's always talking about boys and her friend Kelly who's so perfect. Her laugh gets on your nerves and when she finally gets back on the plane you're almost relieved to see her go.

Fast-forward to next week, when you run into Him at the mall. He has an Eddie Bauer bag—God, He's bought one of those awful shirts again. As He bends to put His bags down you notice, wow, His hair has really thinned out on top. He puts His hand out to touch your shoulder and you notice He's still biting His nails—remember when that noise used to interrupt every video you watched? And then He makes a funny disparaging comment about His family or His new shirt and you remember again why He always made you laugh. Except this time that thought doesn't fill you with longing and it doesn't rip your heart out. When He asks if you have time for a coffee you tell Him truthfully that you don't, and you don't spend another minute trying to figure out when you could get together. You're genuinely pleased to bump into Him like any old friend but genuinely happy to say goodbye.

When you walk down a street you used to walk down together, you suddenly get a glimpse of the old you, your old self that you were in that relationship. You smile like you might when your eyes connect with someone you think you might recognize, someone vaguely familiar whom you want to acknowledge, but you pass by and keep going forward, on with your day.

It's time to remind you of the original bittergirl manifesto that you might have skimmed over way, way back at the beginning of this book. It's the bittergirl Declaration of Independence, the pronouncement we have made to the world.

Everyone has their story.
Some have many stories.
But there's always one:
The one we coin the breakup of all breakups.

And everyone thinks theirs is the most painful.
"Nobody hurt like I did," we say.
We thrive on it, we bond through it.
And if someone steals our glory, if someone's story surpasses the pain
  and hurt of our tale, we dismiss it.
Don't dismiss it.
We've all earned our scars.
Remember, when all hope is lost, when you feel there's no tomorrow,
You're walking in darkness and drowning in sorrow,
Remember,
Yesterday's heartache is tomorrow's one-liner.
We laugh and move on.
It's what we do. It's how we get through.
We've got our stories. What's yours?

Because here's the dish: A bittergirl is not really bitter. She has crawled through the trenches of heartbreak hell and come through seasoned, experienced, wiser, and funnier. She can take on the world again with her sense of humor intact and a raft of good stories to tell.

Well, bittergirl, you've got your own story now. So tell it to the world.

🍸 bitteractivity

There are no exercises. Pour yourself a drink, honey, and kick off your heels. You are so done.